How to Work for a Woman Boss*

*Even if You'd Rather Not

How to Work for a Woman Boss*

*Even if You'd Rather Not

Dr. PAULA BERN

DODD, MEAD & COMPANY
New York

Published by Dodd, Mead & Company, Inc.
79 Madison Avenue, New York, N.Y. 10016
Distributed in Canada by
McClelland and Stewart Limited, Toronto
Manufactured in the United States of America
First Edition

1 2 3 4 5 6 7 8 9 10

Library of Congress Cataloging-in-Publication Data

Bern, Paula.
How to work for a woman boss even if you'd
rather not.

Includes index.
1. Managing your boss. 2. Women executives.
I. Title.
HF5548.83.B48 1987 650.1'3 86-16735
ISBN 0-396-08839-2

Dedication

This book is dedicated with love
to my husband, Joseph Bern,
and to my children, Bruce,
Caryn, Marshall, Sam,
Rona, and Frank.

Contents

Acknowledgments

A special thanks to my husband Dr. Joseph Bern, editor Barbara Beckman, research assistant David Brock, economist Susan Shank, Professor Richard K. Seckinger, and Dr. Dorothy Finkelhor for their never-ending support and understanding.

How to Work for a Woman Boss*

*Even if You'd Rather Not

Chapter 1

Women Managers Invade the Workplace

Sex Roles Upset

Is there a female boss in your future? Absolutely! Will it be your choice? Probably not!

The current unprecedented flow of women into the business world means that one of these days you're going to find yourself in the same situation as Ted, a young petroleum engineer who telephoned me from Houston, Texas. "I need help," he says. "I have a new woman boss, and I find that I have a real hangup about reporting to her. Don't get me wrong, she's damned good—has as much expertise as any guy—even kind of looks like one in her pinstripe suit and matching attaché case, but I feel like I've lost my identity. Sort of out of control. For God's sake, petroleum engineering is a *man's* job! At first, I was so ashamed, I couldn't tell my wife that our project director is a woman. And believe me, my boss sure isn't a mother figure—I tried telling her some of my personal problems one day, and she shot back with 'I can't be bothered with that homefront bullshit. This is the office, and I'm not your wife or therapist.'"

The question of how to work for a woman manager is being asked by thousands of men and women across the nation. It is critical, not only for Americans, but for people in other societies around the globe, where women of many nationalities are moving into the labor force. In Britain, for instance, despite persistent unemployment, women currently make up 42 percent of the workforce—a 5 percent increase, or over a half million more women than were employed in 1971.[1]

Joanna Foster, head of the London-based Pepperell Unit, an organization founded in 1984 to help British employers make better use of the skills of their women employees, says, "Approximately six years ago we began the second phase of our feminist movement, but we still lag behind America in that very few women have made it into management levels and we still don't have the numbers of women working that you do."[2] In the United States at present, 54.1 percent of our adult workforce is female, and 7.9 percent of these employed women are in management positions.[3]

Japan, too, is experiencing a similar dramatic change in their workplace. The most recent statistics indicate that women constitute 35.6 percent of the labor pool while out of the total number of women working, 60 percent are married.[4] According to Yoko Koike, instructor of Japanese at the University of Pennsylvania, "Women in Japan who achieve independence through higher education and their own special talents have an unprecedented choice of life-styles and a wide range of options."[5]

As the numbers of working women increase, it is inevitable that many will progress into various levels of management, for research indicates that women are serious about their careers.[6] Although still considered by some analysts as a "foreign element" in management, women in Britain, Japan, and America are moving upward inexorably into managerial positions. Although women are still concentrated in the lower and middle levels of management in fields that have traditionally employed large numbers of females—health professions, property and real estate, and personnel and labor relations—many talented women now are aiming for top jobs in the professional, business, and corporate worlds. They want to be the new bosses in the executive suite.

Top Leaders Present Their Views

In order to give you an overview of the complex yet fascinating phenomenon of the woman manager today, I contacted such well-known leaders as Prime Minister Margaret Thatcher, former UN Ambassador Jeane J. Kirkpatrick, Professor Peter F. Drucker, Mayor Dianne Feinstein of San Francisco, USAir Chief Executive Officer Edwin Colodny, attorney Bella Abzug, and dozens of other prominent persons from the business, corporate, and political sectors. Determined to obtain the broadest possible perspective on the issue, I also interviewed over two hundred male and female subordinates who now report to woman managers. In return for a promise of anonymity, many candidly related their own experiences with a female boss and offered me their view of the changing workplace.

With more than 55 percent of the female population now part of America's labor force, the workplace of the eighties belongs as much to women as to men—and women bosses are more visible than ever before in our history. In fierce competition for career advancement, women in management are upsetting traditional sex roles. Their behavior in some cases has been inconsistent and confusing—to you, their subordinates and peers. Their ambivalence about how to compete successfully for the managerial suite and how to treat both the men and the women who report to them is setting up formidable obstacles to the advancement of both sexes.

Virginia, a twenty-six-year-old copywriter, may be in Chicago, but she's having the same problems with the altered workplace as Ted, the petroleum engineer in Texas. As we eat lunch together at a deli, she admits, "I don't know how to cope with my senior account exec. At first, I was thrilled when I realized that they were bringing in a woman—the first female manager—in the company. 'Thank God, it's about time,' I said to myself. 'At last a woman role model instead of the guys in their Brooks Brothers getup.' But, boy, was I wrong! She's just a clone of the men. In fact, sometimes I think she's worse. At meetings, she often ignores my suggestions—doesn't even appear to hear them—and points out my past mistakes in front of everyone. She praises the men and puts me down. Why does she treat me like this? Is it possible that it's because I'm the only other woman in the department?"

Yes, Virginia, it's quite probable that your sex has a lot to do with your manager's actions. Dr. Peter F. Drucker, an internationally renowned management consultant and Clarke Professor of Social Science and Management at Claremont Graduate School says, "The greatest complaint I hear from women is that their female bosses tend to be very hard on them. Although competition enters in, I feel that most of the time it's because the woman bosses are trying to prove that they're not showing favoritism to another woman."[7]

As for your female manager not hearing you, she undoubtedly has adopted the listening habits of her male role models. She is "tuning out" what you say and playing the intimidating boss at the same time. It is imperative that you understand that there are only a few places slotted in most companies for women managers, and thus ambitious female subordinates can be perceived as threats.

On the other hand, Ted's reaction to his woman boss stems from his own feeling of anger and insecurity. Reporting for the first time to a woman, he perceives her as invading his field of masculine work—a macho occupation in which he takes pride. Author Anthony Astrachan says:

> Anger is not men's only emotion about women in traditionally masculine fields. . . . they also feel fear, anxiety, envy, shame, and guilt. These feelings produce three patterns of behavior: hostility toward women; denial of women's competence and performance; and the compulsion to transform women, in our heads, into something we can deal with, in order to avoid treating them as peers—into nuns or whores, wives or lovers, daughters or sisters, or mothers.[8]

History in the Making

Both Virginia and Ted are participants in an historic transition in the workforce, in which unforeseen and unresolved issues are emerging as a direct result of the ongoing feminist revolution that started more than two decades ago. "Though the women's movement has changed all of our lives and surpassed our dreams in its magnitude," says Betty Friedan, "we are finding that it's not so easy to live with. . . . The very choices, aspirations, opportunities that we have won for women—no matter how far from real equality—and the small degree of new power women now enjoy, or hunger for, are converging on and into new economic and emotional urgencies."[9]

Developing women managers in the workforce is no longer a "lay back issue," according to organizational analyst Martha G. Burrow. Rather, it is, she says, essential to our society, because the sociological significance of the movement of women into the business world will have an impact on Americans for generations to come.[10] Professor Eli Ginzberg of Columbia University, a former chairman of the National Commission for Employment Policy, maintains, "The single most outstanding phenomenon of our century is the flood of women into jobs." He adds, "This trend is affecting lifestyles, interpersonal relationships, real estate patterns, politics and government, and all aspects of organizational life."[11]

More important, it's affecting *you!* As a subordinate, you know your first reaction when you are told, "Your boss is a woman." The two words *woman boss* carry with them all of the deep-rooted attitudes and gender-related expectations that stem from a traditionally male-dominated workplace. You ask yourself, how can women have learned in a mere twenty years what their male counterparts have been picking up gradually for a period of two hundred years? You wonder if women can, indeed, master the rules of a bureaucratic system—the conduct, procedures, and informal business relationships—that will enable them to reach the top levels of management quickly in order to share the finest and most noble aspects of their traditional sex roles. Will this make it possible, then, for everyone to benefit from the apportionment of power in the workplace?

Attorney Bella Abzug cherishes a vision of the contemporary woman's positive impact on the business world. "I think that women who find themselves in special places where women, traditionally, haven't been before, have a responsibility to change society. I, personally, am not interested in having women in power unless they're going to change the nature of power as it is manifest today in our nation. I believe women should change the nature of power rather than have power change the nature of women."[12]

Males Rule the Workplace

Historically, the business world has been a male bastion. Its style of communication arose directly out of the mode of male upbringing within our society. Women's lack of exposure to that early conditioning played havoc with their ability to compete successfully with each other and with male colleagues during the early years of the feminist movement. In 1977, Professors Margaret Hennig and Anne Jardim of Simmons College identified the lifelong exposure of males to team sports as a major factor in their ability to get along with each other in the workplace:

> As team members, men already have learned the ground rules for relationships among their mostly male colleagues in management. Thus, in the competition for career advancement in the ranks of today's corporate management, men have a clear advantage over women.[13]

As we approach the twenty-first century, the workplace domination enjoyed by the male half of our population has been dramatically altered. Changes in social values and economics, aided by pressures brought by women's groups on the government, the universities, and the corporate structure, have enabled numerous successful women to obtain a piece of the action. With their movement into management, many of these same women no longer want to be affiliated with minorities—the women's groups. They choose instead to be "one of the boys." Male and female roles are blurring in the business world. According to former UN Ambassador Jeane J. Kirkpatrick, "the fundamental qualities for success are identical for both men and women."[14] Don't expect nurturing, caring, or mothering from your new woman boss. Ambassador Kirkpatrick says, "I do not believe there are sex-specific characteristics of an *effective* manager. The qualities a subordinate should expect from *any* boss are intelligence, imagination, hard work and openness."[15] Anthony J. A. Bryan, chairman, and chief executive officer of the Copperweld Corporation, states, "It is completely anachronistic to see women as different than men in the work world. It's merely a matter of time until women reach top positions, for they haven't been a feature that long in the business environment."[16] Norma Pace, senior vice president of the American Paper Institute, maintains, "Being a woman does not provide any special qualities for making a better manager. Female intuition or other sex-related qualities are useful but not significant factors in success."[17]

These candid perspectives of a genderless executive are shared by numerous highly respected persons whom I interviewed. Each one reinforced the need for you to see your manager as neither male nor female but rather as a leader with certain skills and capabilities.

Act Like a Man, Not Like a "Broad"

Many successful women have told me—generally in private—that they feel it is necessary, at this point in time, to imitate the goal-oriented traditional male role model in order to reach a managerial position. And numerous male executives support this premise. Karen Valenstein, first vice president at E. F. Hutton

Company, readily admits that her first mentor, Lewis L. Glucksman, of the Fireman's Fund Insurance Company, warned her during their initial meeting, "I'm not going to pay you like a broad and I'm not going treat you like a broad, so don't act like a broad."[18]

Author Betty Harragan supports this hard-line view, maintaining, "When women had all the time in the world—in the fifties and sixties—to be sweet, nice, feminine—all the nurturing bullshit, it got them nowhere. Now, no one has time for that nonsense. You produce in the business world or you're out."[19]

Some women executives feel they have reached their senior management positions *in spite* of being female. Wenke B. Thoman, vice president for business development and specialty retailing for the American Can Company, says, "Being a woman in business is what I call a 'knockout' factor—something that throws us out of the race to the executive suite. The ones who make it to the top in our society are those who offend people the *least*—in sex, race, appearance, and ability. Those in senior management want women to be men just like them—clones."[20]

One prominent chief executive officer who feels that her femininity is an asset is the outspoken Jane Evans of Monet Jewelers. "Women managers have to 'knock em dead,' " she says with irrepressible humor. "Let's be noticed and never dress like a man. I dress to the nines with great jewelry, naturally! If you've got the position, flaunt it!"[21]

Bonnie Predd, vice president for marketing of Walden Books—and the first woman to achieve that senior position in the company—elaborates: "I don't think women have to become macho in order to make it into top management. You have to have confidence, an awareness of yourself, a real tough skin, and a sense of humor. You've got to prove yourself as a woman manager and when you've done it—to your own satisfaction—you will know you've made it."[22]

With these often conflicting beliefs, what can you, as a subordinate, expect from a woman boss? It's a hard question to answer, for both men and women are experiencing difficulties in reporting to the woman manager. Guidelines for your behavior are nonexistent. Advice is confusing. Your own experience—if any—is limited. As for your woman manager, in many cases she finds herself on a collision course with the men and women under her—yet she doesn't know where her management techniques have failed. With well over a million women entering or reentering the workforce annually,[23] it is obvious that more and more of them are going to seek middle-management positions on an increasingly larger scale. Faced with this reality, it is imperative that you learn how to work for a woman—even if you'd rather not.

No Ground Rules for Women

Interaction between women bosses and their subordinates is a whole new facet of organizational life, and none of us is sure of the ground rules. I first became aware of the need to reevaluate the woman manager's impact on the workplace years ago, when I was offered the position of editor at a West Coast publishing house. Baby-sitter hired, new briefcase tucked securely under my arm, I entered the office prepared to meet my boss—undoubtedly, a male. But instead, I found a woman editor-in-chief. Diane, a petite blonde with a soft, whispery kind of voice, was intelligent, capable, and powerful in a work hierarchy otherwise made up solely of male managers and executives. I was delighted and saw her as a person to emulate in my new career plans.

Diane, on the other hand, seemed wary of me and appeared to view the eleven women subordinates who worked at our firm as possible threats to her solitary position as a woman manager. We were outsiders; she was an insider within the power structure. She seemed to gain personal strength from being a member of the elite male group, copying their mannerisms, their speech cadences, and their subtle put-downs of the women subordinates. Diane was always aloof, conscious of her special status.

Lunch hours found my new boss with the president and other

company executives devising long-range plans in the tastefully furnished corporate dining room. Where was I? In the firm's cafeteria, along with the other women and men still struggling for a toehold on the management ladder. A number of the women ate together, and the conversation often focused on a single topic—Diane.

She was described at various times as "bitchy, too aggressive, overbearing, tough, secretive, and noncommunicative with her female co-workers." By the time we were sampling each other's desserts, all of us had reached a decision: "Diane had to have slept her way to her prestigious position; otherwise, how did she do it?" Or, as one of the copyreaders facetiously put it, "She didn't bring the old man coffee, nor sharpen his pencils, so what the hell else did she do?"

Initially, I joined with my female colleagues in this unfair condemnation of Diane—a superb manager from whom I ultimately learned many of my present managerial techniques. The character traits attributed negatively to Diane by the rest of the women employees became desirable attributes when we applied them to our male bosses. Don was aggressive and authoritative—never overbearing. Ray was not uncommunicative—merely properly closemouthed in respecting the confidentiality of his clients. Peter was ambitious and had fought his way to the top. He hadn't slept his way to the executive suite with the CEO's daughter—he got there by guts and determination. None of the males were ever described as being bitchy. Instead, the women viewed the occasional displays of temper by their male managers as evidence of the executives' total commitment to the company.

Men with Bruised Egos

This hostility toward women in power occurs in both male and female subordinates. It is a psychic barrier to advancement and understanding. Bruised egos abound in epidemic proportions today among male subordinates who report to a woman. The 1985

Virginia Slims American Women's Poll by the Roper Center reveals that 32 percent of working men prefer a male boss—an increase from the 26 percent recorded just five years ago by the same organization.[24] In a 1984 Gallup Poll, more than 41 percent of the senior-level women managers surveyed said they had encountered male subordinates who resisted taking orders from them. Among women bosses who were termed "young achievers" in the same survey, a massive 55 percent said they had experienced resentment from the men who reported to them.[25]

Although analysts have come up with dozens of esoteric reasons for the prejudices revealed by such surveys, the numbers are not suprising. Common sense tells you that as the labor force is inundated increasingly with women, many men will feel threatened on a variety of fronts. In fact, this identity crisis for males has reached such staggering proportions that over one hundred colleges around the country are currently offering courses on such subjects as the psychology of men, male stereotypes, male traumas, and the male experience. "The frontier and soldier images have begun to deteriorate, as has the image of man as breadwinner," explains Dr. Shepherd Bliss, a psychology professor at John F. Kennedy University in Orinda, California. "There is tremendous sadness and loneliness and isolation in being a man today."[26]

In the sixties, American men faced their first challenge with the enactment of equal opportunity laws. Until then, the masculine power structure had been inviolate. No sooner had the potential for the doubling of the competition for each male-held job been established than mothers, daughters, wives, and lovers went after those jobs. The centuries-old tradition of women as nurturers, caretakers, and supporters was assailed on all sides. Myths and stereotypes have by now been shattered and disproven. In a cultural revolution that is still going on, almost 14 million more American women are in the workplace than there were ten years ago.[27] Is it any wonder, then, that with their familiar world—both at home and in the office—turned upside down, some men say they would rather not work for a female boss?

Executive women like Dee Davis Wells, manager of public

affairs for USAir, are fearful that female managers sometimes forget the obstacles they encountered along the way to success. "A change seems to come over women when they hit the executive suite, and they're less supportive of those who report to them. Just when they need the human relations aspect . . . the personal touch . . . many of them lose it. I think it will be another twenty-five years before women learn how to use power properly."[28]

And this means playing the power game as men have done it for decades, says Wendy Reid Crisp, former editor of *Savvy* magazine. "Women have the same talents and skills as men do, but they haven't yet learned how to play the game . . . chalking up the score according to what's going to pay off for them. If a powerful man calls me for a favor . . . perhaps to hire his daughter or wife . . . I'll do it. I *like* to have someone owe me one."[29]

Who Wants to Mentor Women?

As for women executives acting as sponsors or mentors for other women aiming for the managerial suite, the reality is that the amount of assistance you will receive depends upon your female manager's preception of her own struggle to reach the top. If it was extremely difficult, she'll be loath to help others. Felice N. Schwartz, president of Catalyst, says, "The pyramid narrows enormously at the top. We're only now seeing the base from which we will be drawing more women managers each year. At this point in time, there are perhaps only 50 women executives in the same category as Jane Evans; and just another 250 women at the next lower level."[30]

Responses to a recent survey by *The Harvard Business Review* titled "Executive Women—20 Years Later" indicate that the percentage of executives who think women are uncomfortable working for other women has risen dramatically in the last twenty years. The study offers several explanations for what it terms "the apparently growing adversarial relationship between women superiors and their subordinates."[31] Authors Charlotte Decker Sutton and Kris K. Moore suggest:

> In an effort to mold her female subordinates into competent corporate women, the female boss may actually demand more of them. A subordinate may not only resent the additional demands, but also be disappointed at not receiving the warmth, support, and encouragement that female bosses are "supposed" to excel in. . . . Moreover, female subordinates may suspect that a limited number of company positions are open to women and thus feel competitive with their female bosses. Finally, evidence suggests that problems are particularly likely to arise when a younger woman supervises an older woman.[32]

No longer do most women feel that they must be "good girls" and nurture their subordinate "sisters" as extensions of themselves. The mantle of "mentor" has been discarded by numerous managerial women out of necessity, for many of them are pragmatic breadwinners often supporting young children and elderly parents. Is this good or bad? In most cases, it is neither. It is reality. Ms. Crisp explains, "I'm not doing social welfare work . . . that's not my job. I tell young women . . . 'If you want to know what it's like in the magazine business, get a job and start at the bottom.'

"Our big problem as women is that we still have—as in years past—the option *not* to succeed in the world of business. No pressures . . . no one forcing you to be successful . . . so we're not survivalist about our careers. 'Maybe my dad will help, maybe my husband or boyfriend will help.'. . . We have allowed society to impress upon us the belief that we remain subordinates, and have someone take care of us, so we're not fighting our way to the top."[33]

It is clear that the emergence of women bosses in today's workplace is changing far more than the structure of the organization. It is changing our perception of ourselves and our roles in society. How do you feel about reporting to a woman? Are you uncomfortable? What is your unconscious attitude toward your female manager, and how does it match reality? If you're the woman in charge, what kind of guilt trip are you on because you haven't the time or energy to be all the things you are supposed to be—career woman, mother, cub scout leader, chauffeur, cook, wife, hostess, and bed partner? Finally, if you're the woman manager, with few role models to follow, what kinds of new behaviors are you improvising for the workplace? And have you the courage to break the mold if you feel it is necessary? Karen Valenstein, one of the nation's preeminent women in investment banking, makes no apologies for her present inability to be a door-opener for other women on the way up:

> I only deal with the top one percent of career women and I have no use for the rest of them. What I mean is that being a mentor takes a lot of time and I spend my time where it counts. I'm not doing it for anyone I don't have an economic stake in. I'm not in this to be a nice guy; I'm too profit-oriented.[34]

If you are male and working for a woman, the chances are good that you, too, have mixed feelings of confusion and ambivalence about your boss. Dave, a financial analyst for a real estate firm, says he expected understanding from his woman boss, but all he received were orders. "I expected her to be a bit compassionate . . . like my mother, or girlfriend . . . the only women who ever told me what to do. But she's different, and I don't know how to deal with my feeling of uneasiness around her. . . . Maybe I should try to 'make' her. At least I would know the rules there."

Dave's half-humorous, half-serious solution to his initial encounter with a woman in power points up the reason why this book is needed. It is the first book that tells you how to work successfully with the woman manager of the eighties. I advise you how to interact with her professionally, how to behave toward her if you want job advancement, how to protect your flanks and beat her at her own game, and, finally, how to attain a management level without disqualifying the validity of your experience in working with a woman boss.

Can you do it all? Of course! But first you have to take the best from the male and female strengths in the workplace and use them to your advantage. This means that you must abandon any self-defeating and outmoded aspects of your upbringing and be single-minded in adopting the detailed prescriptions for success offered in this book.

I have identified for you the most common negative management styles used by women bosses so that you can develop your own personalized plan for working successfully with your manager. Thus, by studying these stereotypical and ineffective modes of behavior, you can learn the most effective tactics to adopt for your own success.

As an extra boost to your making the grade with your female boss, I have given you more than 240 in-depth coping strategies for virtually all the situations you might face. With these workplace-tested tactics, you will learn what to do when you have a no-management boss, a nonlistening manager, a power broker, an intimidator, and many more.

For instance, in true stories like the one of Dr. Marie Turner, a resident in obstetrics at a Tulsa medical center, you'll learn how to handle an intimidating boss. This young physician told me of her initial encounter with her first woman supervisor, a head nurse in the hospital. Said Dr. Turner, "She ran after me down a long corridor, grabbed my shoulder, and said, 'Why the hell didn't you take that bedpan out of Smith's room? It's stinking up the entire floor and you walk out . . . pleased as punch with yourself for diagnosing the old crock's hiatal hernia. Yeah, I know, Dr. Goodman patted your ass and asked for a date tonight. So you forgot. Just remember, Dr. Goodman takes a feel of every third-year female's behind. It's the same as shaking hands with him—merely an introduction.' "

Whether you are a young man or a young woman entering the workforce for the first time, a recent college graduate, a reentry woman, a displaced homemaker, an eager MBA, a member of the armed forces, or a newly promoted manager, you will find in the following chapters practical and sound advice for dealing with your woman boss, plus a variety of scenes from the new workplace. If you are a woman who harbors dreams of becoming a prison warden, a drug enforcement agent, or a doctor, turn to Chapter 9, on "breakthrough women." Here you will discover fascinating role models if you're seeking an unusual career.

Amidst the humor and pathos of these various case histories, you should find *your* woman boss perfectly described within this book. When you have determined in which category she fits, take the quiz at the end of that chapter, for it will confirm your evaluation of her workplace behavior. Then all you have to do is follow the detailed coping strategies for your guaranteed success with your female manager.

If you have just become a boss yourself, you will gain fresh insight into the many problems facing you from the stories told by new women managers at the end of each chapter. Special strategies for coping with the unexpected obstacles each one encountered will help you through the weeks immediately following your own promotion, and will pave the way for your advancement toward a top executive position in the future.

In order to protect the identity of those persons who requested anonymity in return for their candor during my interviews in different parts of the country, I have, in many cases, changed their names, occupations, and geographic locations.

Chapter 2

The Manager Who Fails to Manage

When Your Boss Doesn't Take the Bull by the Horns

Al ran his hand through his thinning shock of salt-and-pepper hair, absentmindedly pouring a bottle of imported beer into a mug on the Formica tabletop. "I gotta tell you, I was shocked when Gerry became my boss. Don't misunderstand; I like her, she's a great little sport. We've rubbed elbows at a dozen bars, and she can down a coupla screwdrivers with the best of us. But to see her as the guy over me—no way!

"First off, she doesn't manage at all. Can you imagine a boss who leaves the bossing to the people who work for her? She's busy doing her own thing . . . doesn't tell us what territory she wants covered, which clients need servicing, or what the agenda will be at a scheduled meeting. Oh, I know she's probably trying not to come on too strong, but for Chrissake, we can't read her mind. There's no denying that she's a good salesman—why, she sells more oil than three of us put together. But what do you expect? She's a cute chick, and her legs look a hell of a lot better than mine!"

Frustrated and bewildered by the turn of events at his company that brought an entire sales department of thirty men under a woman manager, Al brandishes an unlit cigar at me, trying to make sure that I understand the enormity of this threat to his masculinity. His new boss is not only a woman, he says, but she's a no-management boss to boot. He claims she'll go to any length to avoid overt actions that might make her male subordinates resentful of her. Most of the men who report to Gerry keep their reservations to themselves, but all of them have indicated to their colleagues in the field that selling oil is a man's business and women have no place in it.

"Sure I'm pissed off," says Ed as he swings his six-foot frame into a chair. A forty-two-year-old salesman who covers a tri-state area adjacent to Al's territory, he's cynical. He wants to talk about his experiences with his woman boss. "Pardon the expression, but I've worked my ass off for this company for thirteen years; I know it inside out and backward. I have some good ideas about what can be done to improve the whole organization, not just sales, but I can't get Gerry to sit down and listen to what she calls 'far-out' schemes. She doesn't want anyone to move out of his slot and try something different. Hell, I wouldn't mind learning a little about drilling or the future of the oil business.

"Am I teed off because my boss is a woman?" Ed responds to my unasked question as he stuffs his briefcase with new brochures, preparing to meet some customers. "Probably. But what bothers me more is that she hasn't taken the bull by the horns and become the tough broad that is needed in the fuel oil game. It's competitive, ruthless, and Gerry has to develop a plan of action so the company continues to grow. Sure, it's great that she's the best salesman—hooray for her—but it's time she involved the whole department in a team effort. Y'know, brainstorming, tossing ideas around, going over new goals. She doesn't seem to have a solid understanding of the business, but she has the title and the salary. All of us feel screwed."

Be a Self-Starter: Forget Your Passive Boss

If you were one of Gerry's subordinates, wouldn't you be bitter? They're right—she's not performing like a manager, and in their judgment she ought to shape up or make a graceful exit. But what they don't realize is that when "she sells more oil than three men put together," their boss is hitting the bottom line—making big money for the company. For this reason alone, the president is not going to fire her. On the contrary, she's going to get a raise, and if her subordinates continue complaining, they'll be heading for the door marked "out"—permanently! Despite her no-management posture, Gerry is marked with the stigma of success. In Michael Korda's view, "The successful woman contradicts the male chauvinist's ideas about women in general—the greater her success, the greater his discomfort. . . . Nothing is more difficult for men to accept than that a woman can do what they can, and do it as well or better."[1]

If you're working for a manager like Gerry, there is no magic formula to change your boss's behavior overnight, but there are some positive steps you can take that should help matters.

1. Put together a plan of action, from assisting the clients who you think need some TLC to presenting creative long-term goals for your company. In an offhand manner, hand the list to your manager as a "few ideas for our next staff meeting." Inasmuch as she probably has done nothing, she should welcome your brainstorm.

2. Keep your annoyance with the boss to yourself. Nothing will be gained by discussing her shortcomings with your colleagues. Who knows? One of them might fancy himself a CIA type and report your gripes to the woman in charge or, worse still, to the president. Remember, his only concern is the bottom line.

3. Present her with regular performance reports on your suc-

cess in the field. Although she has not asked for them, she's bound to be impressed. This could also mean a fatter wallet for you when Christmas bonus time arrives.

4. Forget your anger and quit demanding that your boss have qualities that she doesn't possess at the present time. If she's astute, she's going to realize her deficiencies pretty quickly and overcome the problems.

5. Try to support your no-management woman boss as firmly as you would a male manager with the same weakness. Don't band together with your colleagues in a stand-off posture—you versus her. This will worsen the situation, and she might become even more difficult to deal with.

6. If you need a pat on the back and a "well done" from your woman boss, ask for it! No-management bosses don't give one-minute praisings, except on request.

7. Assume the initiative and test the waters for one of your risky ideas. Get rid of your dependence on your manager's actions. At this point in her career, she's not a turned-on boss. Until she becomes one, you had better carry the ball. When she doesn't approve, she'll intercept.

I had to do just that some years ago when one of my junior account executives proposed that my firm throw a lobster-champagne bash for a dozen visiting British businessmen and their wives. He was taking a risk—with the company's money. "Great PR," he says, "they'll never forget us." He was right, they wouldn't. But neither would my treasurer forget that I had okayed the invitation when our cash flow resembled cold molasses. My subordinate had tested the water and fallen in, but his idea still brought results. Instead of lobster and champagne, we had a modest wine and cheese party and managed to acquire two fantastic new clients.

The point is that even a no-management boss, when pushed to the wall by an employee, will react in some way if she feels that her subordinate's actions are inappropriate. She will realize that he has initiated a move and that if there is an adverse effect, it will rebound on her. Most passive managers, you will find, are quite pleased when a subordinate displays what my grandmother used to call "gumption." If I had been a no-management boss (which

I am not), my employee would have gained respect for me on a number of counts: I was watching the store and keeping track of the purse strings, and I showed willingness to go along with an innovative idea. Undoubtedly, if I were a no-management boss I would have given some of my subordinates the idea that I was becoming a "hands-on" boss and emerging from my previous passive state.

8. Assuming that you have a good relationship with your woman superior, tactfully suggest that a few workshops might be helpful for achieving greater understanding between her and the men and women in her department. She may view this as a fine idea and present it to the president. Many excellent training programs are available and are quite effective for lessening a tension-filled workplace atmosphere.

To expedite matters, you might offer to check out the possibilities for your boss. The first step, of course, would be to approach colleges and universities in your town for continuing education programs on management problems. Your next step would be to head for the library and look at the four-volume set of *The Encyclopedia of Associations*. Under the section "Trade, Business, and Commercial Organizations," you will discover literally hundreds of organizations offering a multitude of training programs everywhere in the country. Just a few of the better-known groups that provide this service are: The American Management Association, headquartered in New York; Center for Creative Leadership, based in Greensburg, North Carolina; American Marketing Association, in Chicago, Illinois; Project Management Institute of Drexel Hill, Pennsylvania; and the Institute for Certified Professional Managers, located in Harrisonburg, Virginia.

The Absentee Boss

Trudi makes heads turn as she strolls along Madison Avenue with her long auburn mane swinging in the spring breeze. Her expression is thoughtful when she meets me for brunch to relate her experiences with her first boss—"a woman away from the office so much that several of her subordinates have never spoken ten words to her." Trudi received a degree in math last year. "Cum laude," she tells me proudly. "I was sort of young and naive, so when I was offered a job as a junior accountant—low man on the totem pole—at this medium-size accounting firm, I grabbed it. There are nine of us in the same department—six men and three women—and we really get along well. All except for one problem: a boss who is never there when you want her. Like an absentee landlord, she's an absentee boss."

"Why don't you grab her when she opens the door and tell her you need her?" I ask.

Trudi looks aghast, "Are you kidding? It wouldn't do a bit of good. She wants to hide from the office, get away from the puddles and sandpits we sometimes fall into. When she returns and I ask for assistance, her standard answer is one with which we're all familiar: 'I really want to help you, but I'm swamped with work and should be at a board meeting in fifteen minutes. See if you can figure out a course of action, and when I come in, we'll go over your plan together.' Naturally, when she returns she has a dozen other items on her agenda, and every project is shoved another two weeks into the future."

A Paper Pusher is Not a Manager

Trudi's boss is "fogging" in order not to manage. By hiding behind an impenetrable screen of multiple meetings and mountains of work, she actually avoids being a manager. Oddly enough, her department within the accounting firm functions well; all the highly skilled subordinates take over and produce the jobs on time. They get them done so efficiently that top management is pleased and not aware of the problem. Trudi's passive boss is a paper pusher, a very capable CPA who is turned on by figures, not by people. Moreover, she doesn't want anyone reporting to her who needs supervision. She is fortunate that, except for Trudi, everyone in the department is a self-starter, with enough years of experience to feel confident in their abilities.

For Trudi's peers, their manager's disappearance into the fog is a positive experience. "It's a great work environment," says one of the men at a desk alongside hers. "I can do my own thing and learn from my colleagues." Is this necessarily negative? No, say John Naisbitt and Patricia Aburdene in *Re-Inventing the Corporation*. "The most distinguishing characteristic of the re-invented corporation is that it is a place where employees experience growth . . . where people are talking about their work, exchanging ideas . . . where people are working on what interests them most, although it means stretching to learn new tasks related to your job."[2]

Luckily for Trudi, she realizes that a no-management boss in a loosely run workplace is wrong for her at this time. It's her first job after college, and she hasn't had the experience necessary to be a self-starter. The day we met, she was job hunting; one firm already had made her an attractive offer, and she was investigating several others. Her decision to seek another job is a wise move. As author Betty Harragan says,

> Your most important relationship in any job is the one with your immediate boss. It is critical that you develop as good a working relationship as possible with this person. If that becomes totally impossible, your only option is to get out. Women employees frequently observe or get caught in destructive boss-subordinate situations and are appalled because "nobody will do anything about it."[3]

Speak Up to Avoid Overload

Twenty-seven-year-old Ellen faced a different type of workplace dilemma when I met her in San Jose. An assistant librarian at a small hi-tech corporation, she enjoyed her position until her boss, the head librarian, noted how rapidly she completed her various duties. "One day I came in and found my desk piled about a foot high with work," she says. "First chance I had, I went to her office and asked, 'What gives? When do you want those projects finished?' She said, 'As fast as you can. You evidently have plenty of spare time.' From then on, the job became a nightmare. My boss appears to be sympathetic and blames the 'higher-ups' for the impossible volume of work. If this is true, she should go to bat for me . . . but she's totally detached and refuses to get involved. My deadlines are unrealistic, and the workload is enough for a horse. What shall I do? I think I'm being used."

Ellen is right. She's being taken for a ride. Ellen is being viewed as totally passive, as willing to take any abuse without speaking up, and the manager is taking advantage of the situation. She's neither managing well nor making proper use of Ellen's talents, but on the other hand she has a compliant, easy-to-manipulate subordinate. This affords the passive boss a great chance to avoid managing but to still get the volume of work done. If your manager is pushing you to the wall, try one or two of the following steps:

1. Take a stance—say no, and be consistent. You're going to have to show some aggressiveness, otherwise your no-management boss will assume you can do the work of not one horse but an entire team. Indicate the amount of work you can accomplish within a given time. Stick to it, and don't be forced into taking on more.

2. Ask for a salary increase based on your high-caliber performance. A passive boss usually will not offer you a raise. With the volume of work that you're doing, it is very likely that your boss will reward you, providing you can psych yourself up to request a more impressive paycheck. How you approach your manager is most important, so take heed of the Boy Scout motto and be prepared. Dr. Sharie Crain suggests:

> Make a list over an extended period, of all of your areas of responsibility, the specific duties you perform, and how you allocate your time. Try to establish that, since your present salary was set, you have taken on additional responsibilities, performed them well, and have become a more valuable and well-trained employee of the company. It is a good general rule that the more important you can make your job appear, the greater the compensation man-

> agement will feel it deserves. If you have made specific contributions . . . cite these when you talk to your boss. Try, if possible to quantify the results you obtained, because most managers don't speak English, they speak arithmetic.[4]

3. Should you know of an interesting seminar or a convention where you would have an opportunity to scout new job openings and to meet other professionals in your field, ask your boss if you may attend. A no-management supervisor will never suggest to you that such activities are broadening and helpful. Or that they make you a more valuable employee. Try writing a formal request to her for the time off and for all expenses to be paid by your company.

4. If you have confidence and feel that you're irreplaceable, put in a request for an assistant. Tell your boss that with some help—part-time, if the budget is strained—you'll be on top of each job and exercise tight supervision over all the projects. This logic should appeal to someone who avoids managing, particularly if she is under pressure from her boss to respond more quickly to the needs of everyone in the corporation.

A Good Old Boy in Pantyhose

The down side of hearing about characteristic skirmishes between no-management women bosses and their subordinates is that it might lead you to the conclusion that guerrilla warfare is inevitable in this kind of workplace relationship. But don't despair—it isn't. Generally speaking, a woman supervisor who is afflicted with management paralysis is trying very hard to be a "good old boy" in pantyhose. She goes out of her way to stay out of your office, let alone your hair. Job security is uppermost in her mind, so she worries more about getting along with her own superior than with her subordinates.

Ada-Margaret is a quality checker in a large milk processing plant. As she adjusts her immaculate white cap preparatory to going back to her spot "in line," we talk. She says, "You might call my boss a 'hands-off' sort of manager—totally detached from anything that we're doing—but a really nice woman. We all enjoyed her way of managing until a crisis occurred about a month ago regarding possibly contaminated milk. Then everything hit the fan. As usual, our manager didn't know what was going on; she was out of the plant, and television reporters were trying to question some of us. It was brutal. I could have killed her at the time for being so damned unconcerned; yet she is a very likable person."

According to Dr. Michael V. Fiore and Paul S. Strauss, the no-management or passive boss "generally evolves a classic style of management that enables him to adapt to his feelings of insecurity through withdrawal from the daily objective decision-making of the manager by slipping into the role of coordinator, a neutral referee."[5] Because so many middle-management women are still insecure in the executive suite, a no-management mode attracts them. Thus, they don't make waves, and they're perceived as "good Joes" by co-workers.

A Boss Who Wants to Be Loved

Sometimes a boss wants to be liked by everyone, but that egalitarian approach isn't always the best way to manage. Professor David C. McClelland of Harvard and D. H. Burnham claim, "Nice guys often make bum bosses . . . a boss bent on being loved can cause confusion among employees, plus a drop in morale and output."[6]

But you don't have to be told this, particularly if you already recognize your boss in this chapter. What you need are additional coping tactics to make your job more bearable:

1. Don't force a confrontation with your no-management boss. Your goal should be to help her cope with the demands of her job so that the entire department looks good.
2. Disagree if you want, but do what your supervisor requests.

She may say that she doesn't want "yes men" or "yes women" around, but even a no-management boss prefers that subordinates follow her management plan, no matter what their opinion of it happens to be.

3. Don't kid about her abilities or her management style. You're asking for trouble, and it wouldn't accomplish anything to benefit you.

4. When a mistake occurs on a project in which everyone was involved, your passive boss may attempt to transfer responsibility to a subordinate. You don't want to be that subordinate, so be prepared. Document your routine and meetings in a private diary. At least you'll be able to say with conviction, "I had to go to Safesville to service the XYZ account, so Jim Reddy offered to assume authority for that project. Ellen, the project coordinator, has my memo and all the pertinent files. You might check with her and Jim to see what occurred." In polite circles, this is known as CYA—covering your tail.

5. Be enthusiastic and optimistic. These two personality traits will take you far with very little effort on your part. Moreover, they will make you visible, especially when your passive boss practices being invisible.

6. Provide service of such high quality for your clients that your actions generate unsolicited referrals. When a client asks specifically for you, word gets around to senior management, as well as to your boss. Flattering requests for your skills might prompt your manager to be more active and to participate in the day-to-day operations of your department.

7. List both the advantages and the disadvantages of staying in your present position. Is the no-management style of your boss so affecting you that a move is necessary? If it is, plan some long-term goals based on a job change. If not, then devise ways in which you can learn to handle the stress inherent in your present position, and then move forward in your career.

8. Attempt to identify a mentor within your firm. Your passive boss is not the ideal person for this because she is inwardly directed and totally concerned about her own job security.

9. If your boss is the token woman manager within the company, practice patience. She might be acting passive deliberately in order to not make waves or call attention to herself. If you are a woman, remember an important point: businesses that have appointed one female manager are often slow to promote another woman to an equal position. Play it cool; otherwise you will threaten not only your woman boss but her male superiors as well. Your turn will come, either with this firm or with another.

10. Relieve your manager, as much as possible, of making day-to-day decisions. Try to offer her objective and sound solutions; put them in the form of an interoffice memo, and ask her respectfully to initial those that she views as feasible. Then have her secretary return the answers to your desk. Keep copies in a special file. For your short-term career plans, these suggestions, when implemented, will demonstrate your valuable contribution to the company. In the long run, the initiative you've shown will speed up your advancement—away from your passive boss.

An SOS from a No-Management Boss

Now that you have met a number of frustrated subordinates who claim that they're being hung up in their jobs by a female manager in a state of paralysis, it's time to introduce you to Gerry. A dynamo of a woman, she typifies many of the no-action women managers that I interviewed across the country. She is, as you'll recall, Al and Ed's boss in the oil company. Her side of the story illustrates how you, too, could become—inadvertently—a no-management boss.

"I've been a boss for over five months," she says, "but most of the time I feel like a failure, a total wipeout." With a wry grin and a lift of her dark brows, she confesses, "It would kill me if I have to fire anyone. Would you believe that I can't give orders to a cleaning woman, let alone fire her? I'm a real wimp. And here I've done everything a woman is supposed to do in today's world. I've accomplished. I've achieved. For God's sake, I've almost reached the top of the mountain at the age of thirty-seven. I'm sales manager of the company, third from the president, and ever since I got this promotion, I've been scared shitless!"

This startling comment from Gerry, with her tousled, sun-streaked short hair and slim, athletic build, is completely out of character. She's gutsy, with lots of self-assurance.

Why Is She a No-Management Boss?

We're on the way to Gerry's private club in her company car, a luxurious "perk" with a burgundy leather interior that sets off her tanned good looks, when she blurts out her innermost fears. Quickly checking with her secretary on the car phone, she pulls the Porsche into a personalized space in the parking lot and fills me in on her career.

"I thought it would be real cool to be a manager," she says, "but it's not what it's cracked up to be when you don't have the training or self-confidence to carry it through. I had worked for my company almost five years when I was moved 'upstairs.' Next stop is vice president for sales, but I think I need some extra survival gear for that trip."

Gerry laughs as she reminisces about the years she spent as a volunteer with an arts organization, never earning a penny despite her superb fund-raising and organizational skills. "My career started accidentally," she explains. "I managed to wangle a huge grant for my arts group from this guy who turned out to be the president of a small petroleum company. He said, 'Gerry, if you could get a donation of $40,000 out of me when I've never given a nickel to the arts, you would make one hell of a salesman. How about it? Want to work for me?' I looked him in the eye and said, 'Why not? I know I'm smart and capable, and selling diesel oil sounds like fun.' So he hired me, and I had a ball; that is, until I got the promotion. Then I found I was afraid to be a boss."

Gerry says she works for a jobber, buying refined oil from large companies and selling it to "the little guys" at coal mines, barges, construction sites, and wherever diesel fuel is needed. She adds, "I deal in a totally man's world, and my customers are great. They treat me like a lady. Why, they'd die before they would swear in front of me. I sell like crazy—taking a lot of business away from our competitors. I don't see another female salesman in a year of Sundays, and my customers say they would just as soon buy their oil from me instead of a man because I give them a lot of attention. They love me. I'm feminine, not threatening or bullying. I tease them a lot, and they like my breezy style. The problem is, this style doesn't translate well to management. And, boy, I've found that out the hard way."

Thirty men report to Gerry. That responsibility made her plead with the company president, "Hire some guy in my place. I don't think I can hack it as a boss." But, she says, her mentor kept encouraging her with reassuring comments like "You have it in you. You're going to be an excellent executive. Just keep up the steady improvement."

She reflects quietly, "The president is right. I *am* learning how to manage. The guys who work for me are starting to realize that I'm not a ding-dong. Don't misunderstand, the problem is not with them, it's with me. The inner struggle I'm having with myself over how to be aggressive; how to motivate without coming on too strong, without being 'that impossible bitch.' I don't want them to hate me; remember, they're all bigger and tougher than I am. The next salesman I hire will be ten years younger and two feet shorter than I am."

Chuckling at her own joke, Gerry motions for me to follow the maître d' to her reserved table in the club dining room. "You must realize," she says as she sips Perrier water, "I was one of the guys. Perhaps if I had taken the job with the idea that I was going to be a manager, I would have acted differently. But I was on the same level as the men; we shared beers and jokes together. There was no distance between us, so now that I'm in charge, they deny—even to themselves—that I'm their boss. And I've been afraid to give them any orders. But things are changing; I think I'm ready to start acting as the boss."

Tactics to Show You're the Boss

Have you ever encountered this problem—the exciting promotion to your first management position and then the frightening realization that you don't feel mentally prepared to handle the job? Gerry's dilemma is not gender-specific. Men, too, can become no-management bosses, overwhelmed by the unfamiliar demands of a supervisory position. But women are more vulnerable to it, for they tend to see their careers in terms of personal growth, satisfaction, and self-fulfillment. Margaret Hennig and Anne Jardim report that male workers view a career as a series of jobs, "a progression, a path leading upward with recognition and reward implied."[7] A promotion can put women who have neither identified their professional goals nor planned their growth strategies in the workforce into a state of no-management paralysis.

How do you, as a brand-new boss, get out of this passive, unproductive condition? According to the woman managers I spoke to, a few simple strategies can be very helpful:

1. Make sure that your boss clarifies your new position to the rest of the company's employees. This might avert an uproar and will help defuse the inevitable envy of your former peers.
2. Politely request some simple public relations—a companywide memo, a news release to the local paper, and a short article about your promotion in the corporation's house organ. These are a great ego booster and a shot in the arm for your credibility.
3. Have a meeting with your boss and discover the extent of your authority. Are you a paper tiger, or can you hire, fire, and promote? Without visible authority, you haven't any power.
4. Try to become less self-oriented and more company-oriented. This means you will assume tighter control and won't let your subordinates drift off doing their own thing.
5. Become more assured in your power to exercise authority

by associating with other managers. You're now in a formal boss/subordinate relationship with your former peers, which means that you have to withdraw from your previous social activities with them—lunches, after-work drinks—and form new relationships with executives or managers on your own level. This doesn't sound very democratic, I'm aware, but face facts—you went uppercrust when you left the subordinate ranks. This can be painful at first, says Betty Harragan, for "it means going against your spontaneous instincts to maintain personal equality when, in fact, you are now in an elitist situation by virtue of your functional superiority."[8]

6. In order to get out of your no-management mentality, work to increase the power you have within your company. According to Dr. Rosabeth Moss Kanter, "Women managers should analyze which lines of supply, information and support are available to them in their jobs and systematically seek to improve them—partly by 'creative trade,' by beginning to use what resources they do have to build exchange relationships that net eventual gains."[9]

7. As a newly promoted manager, attempt to make yourself part of the informal as well as formal relationships within your company. In other words, become a part of the loose grapevine that exists in all workplaces, so that you aren't excluded as an outsider because of your new role.

8. "Become a team player and bring along the bench or second string," advises Corinne C. Turner, president of Alvin Products, Inc., of Worcester, Massachusetts. "As women managers we tend to stay in a holding pattern, for we're afraid to be vulnerable. It takes courage to act, to bring others along with us and to succeed in our present position so that we can target the next job up. You must realize as a new boss, that you're surrounded by sharks—both male and female—so you have to take charge if you want to progress."[10]

Boss Assessment Questionnaire: The No-Management Mode

Evaluate your boss for a no-managment style with the following rating scale:

A—Always or yes	5 points for each A answer
S—Sometimes or occasionally	3 points for each S answer
R—Rarely or never	1 point for each R answer

1. Does your boss spend a great deal of time away from the office, assuming that a department can run itself? ______

2. When conflicts occur in your division, does she usually let the "troops" resolve the problems among themselves, rather than offer guidance or leadership? ______

3. Does your manager assign you or your peers to keep track of the everyday problems inherent in any workplace—absenteeism, unexplained tardiness, personal issues, or bickering among different subordinates? ______

4. Does your manager avoid setting short-term and long-term goals for your department? ______

5. Does your boss prefer to "do her own thing" while her subordinates drift in other directions? ______

6. Does your manager avoid appraising performances of her people in order to avoid confrontation and discipline sessions? ______

7. Is your manager more likely to choose a tried and true approach to a project than to attempt a new and riskier manner of doing it? ______

8. Does your boss ask her subordinates to check on whether jobs are moving smoothly instead of reviewing the projects herself? ______

9. When your manager's supervisor asks for her personal progress reports on your department, does she pass the assignment on to a subordinate? ______

10. Does your manager avoid thorny issues within your department so that she always appears to be the charming, well-liked administrator? ______

11. Has everyone in your department been warned by your boss not to disturb her outside the office, even for a major crisis? ______

12. Does your boss appear to dislike giving direct orders or applying pressure to a subordinate to get better job performance? ______

Total Score ______

60–45 You have a no-management boss.
44–29 Your boss shows some inclination to manage.
28–12 Congratulations! You have a boss who wants to manage.

Chapter 3

The Woman Power Broker

The Image Is of a Driven Male

Power! The word itself elicits ambivalent reactions from virtually all of us. If we are honest with ourselves, we are both attracted to and repelled by it. Our fascination with the concept of power turns autobiographies of powerful individuals like Mayor Edward Koch of New York and auto magnate Lee Iacocca into overnight best sellers. We loathe the idea of power instinctively as one of the baser needs of mankind when we witness its misuse by a Jean-Claude Duvalier or a Ferdinand Marcos. In all instances, our perspective on power has been historically derived from the men who wield it.

It is only very recently, with the emergence of world leaders like Margaret Thatcher and the late Indira Gandhi, that society has begun to acknowledge that women, too, can desire power, strive for power, and on rare occasions even acquire national power. The issue that must be dealt with in the coming decades is how women use power. Although there is no firm consensus among behavioral scientists on the difference between male and female power styles, my own research has led me to the conclusion that women wield power in very much the same way as men. Or as Katharine Graham of *The Washington Post* says,

> Power has no sex. Ambition and aggression are not masculine characteristics. Sensitivity and consensus-building are not female traits. Women must be willing to embrace all of these qualities—and use them to gain power.[1]

Just how valid these comments are is pointed up by a recent conversation I had with Linda, a senior vice president for sales of a major computer firm in the Southwest. We met in her wood-panelled office whose expansive windows overlook downtown Phoeniz thirty stories below. Having just returned from Majorca, she is relaxed, not yet psyched up for the stressful job that takes her to meetings all over the country. Seventy-five men and women report to her, and her salary is well into the six-figure range. But Linda says she is desperately unhappy. "My boss is an incredible, awesome person. She is one of the ten most powerful women in the country, and we have been friends for many years, but I can't take it any more. Because she is such a winner, she's held up as an example of what a woman executive should be, so that no other woman ever could compete with her."

Linda's long slim fingers fidget aimlessly with a letter opener. She's obviously agitated, and I'm confused. "What on earth is wrong? Your boss sounds like a fabulous role model for you. Why the problem?"

Her chair does a fast 180-degree spin, and she almost glowers at me. "Don't you understand? My achievement level would be far more respected if my boss were a man! She has all the male qualities. She is utterly driven, incredibly aggressive, and totally focused in on herself. She doesn't see anyone else. She is the only one who counts.

"Because I'm disenchanted with her doesn't mean she isn't a wonderful person, but her life, her judgment—everything is governed by her job. And she gets all the credit for the company's success. Never once has she said, 'I could never do this without the incredible support of those who work for me.' "

I ask softly, "Are you jealous?"

Linda looks up with a wistful little smile. "Absolutely."

Women Must Be Like Men to Compete

Linda's boss is a relatively unfamiliar breed of managerial woman—the power broker. Until the last decade, this appellation—which is by no means negative—has been applied solely to men. In fact, males who display an intense power orientation have traditonally been held in high esteem by their colleagues. Perhaps Meg Greenfield, editor of *The Washington Post* editorial pages and a *Newsweek* columnist, expressed it best when she said, "When men are exercising authority people say, 'the old man is really sore today' with great admiration. And when the female behaves in precisely the same way, they say, 'that bitch is probably having a hormonal attack or something."[2]

Hormonal attacks notwithstanding, a woman must assume the same managerial posture as her male counterpart if she is going to compete with him for the executive suite. Dr. Eli Ginzberg, director of the Conservation of Human Resources Center at Columbia University and former chairman of the National Commission for Employment Policy, puts it bluntly: "Our environment determines our behavior. In order to compete successfully in American society, blacks have to be like whites, and women have to be like men."[3]

How difficult it is for some people to accept the latter is pointed up by Jeanne's story. "I'm a writer and during the height of the women's movement, I worked at a feminist magazine in San Francisco. It was thrilling. It was owned by women, run by women. . . . The contents of the magazine were intelligent, informed. I always felt offended by the female putdown in magazines like *Redbook* and *McCall's*. Here was a magazine that spoke to me as a person. And my co-workers were wonderful; someone cared if I had cramps or if I was low on funds. I loved it."

As Jeanne speaks to me, her face glows. She's animated and excited, remembering the seventies. "Then I left the magazine," she continues, suddenly somber and withdrawn. "I was hungry for men in the workplace. . . . It was too much—all women all day. I was longing for men to talk to, to go out with, to do anything with! Now I'm an editor with a hotel trade journal, and my boss, the editor-in-chief, is a woman. She knows how to play the power game brilliantly. She's overly ambitious, overly aggressive. I need balance in my life. I would choose to go to the ballet or the theater before I would choose to entertain a client, but not my boss. Oh, no! She's unrelentingly narrow. Business must come first—over everything.

"All of us have to follow her lead—in at seven in the morning, out at ten or eleven at night. She's always fearful of acceding to her subordinates' wishes—for an extra vacation day, for instance—for if she makes a bad judgment call, and her chief executive officer finds her out, she could be in trouble. So she never leaves herself open. . . . She never makes a mistake. That's the way she plans her career and covers her ass."

Are You Guilty If You Want Power?

My curiosity is piqued. I ask Jeanne the question that has been nagging at me since we began our interview: "Do you hate women?" She looks startled. "Oh, no! No, no! I would rather *always* work for a female. I'm a dyed-in-the-wool feminist, but it's this whole new attitude that women like my present boss have. She's very, very smart, superconfident, egocentric. It robs her of her humanity. Do you think she would ever make an emotional decision? Of course not! But I make emotional decisions all the time, and so do most people."

Jeanne lights another cigarillo; it's her fourth since our conversation began in this small pizza parlor in downtown Denver. She tosses her shoulder-length dark hair back from her forehead, conscious of the gaze of two young men trying to catch her eye from a nearby table. "Here, isn't he cute?" She hands me a snapshot of an impish child of about six. "It's my little boy, Robbie. Perhaps he's one of the reasons why I'm so ambitious. I want to succeed. Like my boss, I'm demanding and tough. But you have to be a noncompetitive robot to survive around someone as focused on power as she is. She really is no different than the men who strive for power. I'm not sure that I have it in me to be like that."

One point still disturbs me about Jeanne's description of the management style of her boss and its effect on her personal life. "Does she feel guilty, do you think, about wanting power so much?" I asked. Jeanne laughed so heartily that she spilled her coffee over a portion of my mushroom pizza. "Are you serious? Is Lee Iacocca ashamed of being power hungry? Heck, no! My boss feels she has the best life in the world."

Evaluate Your Power Drive

The yearning for power exists in all human beings in some degree. It is a basic human drive, but most of us are loath to admit—even to ourselves—that we play the power game often at the expense of others. As the German philosopher Heinrich von Treitscheke explained,

> Your neighbor, even though he may look upon you as his natural ally against another power which is feared by you both, is always ready, at the first opportunity, as soon as it can be done with safety, to better himself at your expense. . . . Whoever fails to increase his power must decrease it, if others increase theirs.[4]

If you, like Linda and Jeanne, have a power broker for a manager, the reality is that with each new aspect and symbol of power gained by your boss, your own power diminishes. This means that you must act quickly to assess your power needs so that you can formulate the psychological tactics that will gain you *real* power.

Ask yourself the following questions. If you answer them affirmatively and unashamedly, without perceiving any negative connotation to your response, you have a great need for power and you should "go for it."

1. Do you view power and leadership as necessary for happiness and satisfaction in your career?
2. Do you like to dramatize yourself and your actions so that you stand out from the crowd at even the most mundane event?
3. Are you willing to accept visibly high-risk assignments from your boss?
4. If you are a woman, are you ready to use your sexuality and femininity as a weapon in your desire to gain power? The choice of weapon, naturally, is yours—from a warm smile to a warm bed.
5. Are you willing to master the hard skills necessary for the power game—negotiation, decision making, risk taking?
6. Can you say no to someone when you feel that a refusal is in your self-interest but not in his or hers?
7. If necessary, can you be shameless in making someone else feel guilty for a mistake that you made, a promise you couldn't keep, or a negotiation that, on second thought, appears unwise?
8. Are you willing to accept failure, humiliation, or defeat in pursuit of power?
9. Would you feel comfortable using power plays such as

- Deliberately arriving late for a meeting in your office that you yourself had scheduled for a specific time?
- Accepting several telephone calls while a subordinate sits patiently on the other side of your desk yawning at the ceiling, and reassuring him, "Be right with you—must finish this important business with Honolulu"?
- Asking your secretary to route all phone calls to a corporate lunch so that you're paged three times between the vichyssoise and filet of sole? To add to the drama, you can request that the phone be brought to your table.

10. Do you crave lavish symbols of power in the workplace like

- A lock on your private telephone?
- A wall clock with time and dates for major cities around the globe?
- An exercycle discreetly tucked into a corner of your inner suite?
- A small refrigerator and bar for in-office toasts?
- A complete shower/makeup area as a part of your office suite?
- A chauffeur-driven limousine equipped with phone, bar, and television set?
- Custom-designed office furniture styled especially to your taste?
- Original oil paintings—massive, naturally—chosen to complement the office decor?
- An elegantly furnished penthouse suite in your office building to accommodate corporate gamesmen who arrive on the Concorde for a morning meeting? After they helicopter out, you can take your siesta in the same plush quarters.
- A company jet so you don't have to travel with the unwashed mob?
- Membership in exclusive private clubs as well as golfing privileges at the plushest country club?

Dr. George L. Peabody, president of Associates for Creative Leadership, Inc., in Washington, D.C., and a recognized expert on power in organizations, takes this perspective:

> Power is the ability to get done what you want done. It demands a pragmatic, cold inhuman eye that can look at things functionally; to see how things actually work. Morality, value, ideology, myth and all human needs, feelings, and loyalties must be temporarily suspended. There is no room for them during power analysis, because they dim the eye of the beholder. Perceive inaccurately and you cannot act effectively.[5]

Coping with a Power-Hungry Boss

After you have evaluated your own personal power drive, you're going to know whether you want a shot at the topmost rung of the ladder. If you do, no one has to tell you that it will be an arduous trek, particularly because there will be power brokers all along the route. If you have a power broker now for a boss, prepare for the climb with a few of the following tactics:

1. Become very aware of your own limitations; evaluate whether you are a "stayer." If you're honest with yourself—with no possibility of imaginary sand castles toppling around your head—then plot your course carefully. The critical question is whether *you* think you're good enough to reach the level you want and to stay there. This means critical self-analysis and total honesty.

2. Decide how long you want to remain a satellite of your woman boss. If your job provides a rich and varied learning experience, it might be worthwhile to stick around. One successful executive told me he spent two years with a power broker who taught him all he knew about "power games." He says, "I needed to learn how to control my own life, and she taught me every trick she used for power-brokering amidst rough competition. To cope with her power ploys at the office, I had to put her out of my mind and give my complete attention to the job at hand."

3. No matter how tough the situation gets, retain your sense of humor. According to business consultant Letitia Baldrige, this is "the one essential character trait that both men and women must have in order to succeed."[6]

4. Be careful of sending defensive messages to your boss. With a power broker for a manager, it is natural for you to anticipate threat in almost any of her actions. But if you are defensive, you hear every sentence she utters as a personal attack on you. Your boss may say, "Joe, do you have the completed schedule for the Falldown Bridge project?" It's a simple request, but you react

angrily, "How could I possibly have finished it this fast? You assigned it to me only nine days ago!" You have become defensive over a simple question, when in reality your boss isn't accusing you of anything.

5. Learn to pick up on your manager's nonverbal messages. This is crucial when your boss is a power broker, for she often feels a tremendous inward urgency about something but tries not to show it to her subordinates. You then must pay attention to the nonverbal message.

Manager: We probaby don't have to worry about this project for another month, so don't push yourself. (Nonverbal tip-offs: She's shaking one foot, frowning at the ceiling, tapping a pen against her desk clock, and shuffling through the project proposal on a corner of her desk.)

You: Shelving it temporarily might be a good idea, but you seem a bit uptight about my getting on with it. Maybe it's just my imagination, but would you feel better if I gave it a priority rating and started the ball rolling?

With this offhand guess, nonthreatening to your high-powered boss, you have given her the opportunity either to agree with your surmisal or to deny your interpretation of her nonverbal communication.

Prime Minister Thatcher's Use of Power

Should you become intrigued by the power game, always remember to evaluate the prevailing conditions, including the forces for and against your actions, before you make a move. This type of pragmatic approach is a hallmark of Margaret Thatcher, the British Prime Minister, considered by many to be the most powerful woman in the world. "She is like Queen Elizabeth I in her use of power. If someone gets in her way, she has little hesitation about getting rid of him," says David Boddy, former director of press and public relations for the British Conservative Party and press secretary to Prime Minister Thatcher during the 1979 and 1983 election campaigns.[7] "Mrs. Thatcher does her homework, she knows the right questions to ask, and she doesn't ever tolerate any foolishness," he adds.

As for Mrs. Thatcher's own perception of her power position on the world stage, Boddy says she sees herself as a CEO (chief executive officer), often commenting to friends, "I'm running Great Britain, Limited." He continues, "Some say she is domineering or hectoring, but because she has so much power, many people misunderstand her. Where she really excels is when someone has the courage to speak up and challenge her. She doesn't back off at the moment, but she will think it over, and if she believes it's a good idea, she'll quietly implement it and later thank the person for the suggestion."

I couldn't resist asking Mr. Boddy, "How did you like working for a woman?" He appeared astonished. "It never entered my mind—that wasn't the primary consideration. I was dealing with the Prime Minister of Britain."

What about the popular belief that those engaged in power games are cold, detached individuals? Mr. Boddy says admiringly of Mrs. Thatcher, "The human aspect is one of her greatest strengths. With the people who work most closely with her, she will relax in the evening, kick off her shoes, and pour the drinks. If you are near the age of her children, as I am, she becomes absolutely maternal."

Maternal Doesn't Always Equal Boss

Undoubtedly, "maternal" is an endearing description for a woman of the Prime Minister's stature when she relaxes and sheds the trappings of power. But for most women who have achieved some managerial status, the label "motherly" is neither welcome nor always intended as admiring. The history of American business is replete with admirable, paternal men, from the mentors who take young men and women under their wings and point them on the road to success, to the executive father figures for the women in the secretarial pool. But mother figures in the power seat of organizations or of corporations have been—and still are—as rare as condors in the wilds. Maternal doesn't equal power in Western societies, except in the kitchen or nursery. The majority of career women try to avoid the label unless they're at the very top and can afford to be amused by it—or flattered by the term's implication of power within the family.

Ellen Gordon, president of Tootsie Roll Corporation, a family-owned company since 1923, is boss to over a thousand men and women, both here and abroad.[8] She says, "I believe that my employees see me as both a maternal figure and as head of a large company. Part of it is because we have an open-door policy—it's very expedient—and anyone can stroll in and out of my office for advice. We're in the southwest of Chicago, a traditional, heavily ethnic area where most of our employees are used to women with power—but only in the home. So they bring me their health problems, their children's troubles, their marital woes. I don't mind, because I *am* a mother, with four daughters, and many of the skills I gained as a homemaker are the same talents that I use in the workplace."

A confirmed workaholic who views weekends as "just two more workdays," Ms. Gordon admits to some discomfort in functioning at an epicenter of power. She has held the title of president for eight years, and she says candidly, "At times, I'm a bit concerned about the tremendous power inherent in a position like mine. People don't dare contradict me, or at least they're often afraid to. The policeman on the beat knows me. . . . The ticket agents at the airport recognize me. . . . The checkout ladies at the supermarket call me by name. I've concluded that the only way to deal with power is to be comfortable with it. You have to be able to sit back and laugh at yourself. If I were to give advice to a woman who is newly appointed to a leadership position, I would say, 'Don't think in terms of male or female when you look at the responsibilities of your job. That will frighten you!' I purposely never think of my gender at the factory, but I also don't believe that women should try to be men when they become managers."

Who Says Tough Guys Can't Be Nuns?

A singular group of women who have adopted the hard-driving aggressiveness of the "tough guy," according to scores of subordinates whom I interviewed for this book, are the nuns in top-level administrative jobs from New York to California. Concentrated in Catholic colleges and hospitals, they have personified for a large segment of the population over the centuries all of the compassionate, gentle, nurturing, and submissive aspects of womanhood. But no more, say their subordinates from a variety of institutions.

"First, let's set things straight," says Dr. Albert Bedell, a highly respected urologist with a large hospital in the Northeast. "I am not antinun, and I'm not antiwoman. The sister who preceded our present administrator was a fine, humanistic individual. She went out of her way to visit patients and talk kindly with the doctors. And it wasn't because she was an old-fashioned nun; she was very secular. In fact, she brought in hairdressers to give hairdos to some of our depressed women patients.

"But she retired, and now we're under the thumb of a new nun-administrator who is playing power games with all of us. She's a different breed—money-minded, gung-ho to put the doctor in his place—going through difficult passages in her own life. We would all like to tell her to go screw off, but you can't say that to a woman, let alone a nun. Meanwhile, she badgers us, tries in every way to put down all of the male physicians and technicians. She wants to be in the limelight when things go well at the hospital, and when there is a problem, she passes the buck on to the doctors. I'm ready to take early retirement if this keeps up."

Looking at Dr. Bedell, it is difficult to imagine anyone forcing him to do anything other than what he wants to do. A big man with a florid complexion and round cheeks reminiscent of Old Saint Nick, his most arresting feature is his large, dark, shoe-button eyes. He speaks slowly and deliberately, anxious to make sure that I don't misinterpret his viewpoint. "I don't believe that my boss wants to control huge numbers of people or even to expand the hospital facilities. What she wants is personal power—to demonstrate her worth to the institution's board of trustees."

Author Michael Korda offers some insight into this type of power game:

> Those who desire personal power are very different. Instead of controlling a portion of the existing world, they set out to create their own. A well-known motion picture director once told me, in all seriousness, that when he made a movie he was God. "I have the world in my hands," he said. "I can make it come out any way I want, decide who lives and who dies, who gets punished, who gets to live happily ever after. In between pictures is my seventh day, I rest." This is, of course a somewhat romantic and self-indulgent view of power. . . . Still, it's a common enough view—those who aren't satisfied with power over things want to create complete worlds that are reflections of their own power. Nothing will satisfy them but omnipotence.[9]

Can Role Expectations Be Wrong?

In the case of this nun-supervisor who exercises power over her subordinates, the frustration of the doctors and the hospital staff is understandable. We have all been conditioned over the years to expect what psychotherapist Rollo May calls "nutrient power" from the female. The perception is that she nurtures and cares for others.[10] When she is a member of a religious order, our expectations of her warmth and "giving" qualities increase. How, then, can we even conceive of a nun playing the power game?

According to Professor David C. McClelland of Harvard University,

> Women's behavior is shaped by role expectations rooted in history and society, and power motivation expresses itself in terms of how women are expected to behave. Because their role had traditionally been to manage social and emotional resources in the family, women are interdependent and especially interested in people and the life process.[11]

In our highly competitive society, where the pyramid of power narrows drastically toward the top, the nun-boss is playing a familiar power game—familiar, that is, to most males in corporate hierarchies, but not to those who work in a service organization. We expect to find master players of the power game among friends and acquaintances who perfect intricate maneuvers in their encounters with IRS agents, state troopers, politicians, or an array of lovers. But to discover *nuns* using power moves in a traditionally masculine way is unthinkable! Determined to keep their positions secure in the complex hospital setting where the male doctor figure has historically been dominant, some nun-administrators use what Dr. May calls a "third kind of power"—competitive power, or power against another. "In its negative form," he explains, "it consists of one person going up not because of anything he does or any merit he has, but because his opponent goes down."[12]

Although we may decry—even condemn—the moves made by this type of female manager, the blunt truth is, as Michael Korda says, "in a competitive world it is necessary to seize every possible advantage, and to learn how to find and secure one's own power spot."[13] He adds,

> Once we understand the nature of the power relationships around us, we can begin to find our security in fluidity and movement, understanding that power is not static, but must be sought, defended, increased and protected by cleverness and originality.[14]

The Power Game in the Halls of Ivy

Sister Hilda, the president of a respected Catholic women's college in New England, is a confident chief executive who follows Korda's premise that power must be protected. A round, cushiony figure with the placid, unlined face of a woman who has spent twenty years in the womb of convent life, she plays the power game with the consummate skill of her male role models, the priest-administrators of the diocese.

How does she accomplish this feat in a hierarchy where genuine power is totally masculine? Where the authentic symbol of authority is a man? "Very easily," says Father Edwin, vice president for development at the college. "My boss excludes everyone in our department from important meetings that affect the fund-raising efforts of the school. She claims that she can accomplish more alone. Naturally, we all know that's an excuse. What she is doing is keeping the power centralized in her office."

Another member of the development department is also disgruntled with the president, for he feels that his efforts are going unrecognized. "Just a few months ago, I managed to obtain a large grant for the college. . . . It was exciting . . . particularly because it came from a foundation that had never responded to us before. I was elated. . . . I thought it would mean some recognition for me . . . Even a pat on the head. But nothing happened. Then I heard through the grapevine that the president claimed credit for the coup when she met with our board. What a lousy deal. I work my butt off, and she gets the applause."

Unfortunately for the faculty members, they are locked into the president's not-so-subtle power game. Dr. Mavis Jackson, president of the Faculty Senate, is perturbed because the boss is infringing on her territory. Dr. Jackson is a secular woman, given to dressing in bold reds and blues, which stand out vividly against the muted shades worn by the nuns, who are newly emerged from their habits. She expresses outrage at "that woman." "Can you imagine a president who insists on attending every committee meeting held by the faculty—on no matter what? I consider it a personal affront . . . an intrusion on my territory. For heaven's sake, she's spying on me! I look ridiculous to our faculty members. She denigrates my authority. She's a woman and a 'religious'; she should bring the human side to management and not act so damned controlling."

Strategies Against Power Plays

Regrettably, this type of manager is not going to change her style now that she has reached the summit. She is a person with immense power needs; thus, she is most likely to continue trying to control all of her interactions with subordinates. The ultimate power broker, with a direct, aggressive approach to management, she will use every bit of power she can muster—authorized or not—to accomplish the job as she feels it must be done. To cope with her, you might experiment with these guidelines:

1. Forget your role expectations for a woman boss involved in power games. Whether or not she is functioning as a member of a religious order is completely immaterial. The important point to remember is that you are dealing with a woman who relishes her power and who is determined to use it to her advantage. Understand this, and you will be able to relax and observe her in action. Meanwhile, you can think fondly back on the good old days when women acted like women!

2. Analyze your manager's power plays to see where she's coming from. If you possess another form of power, figure out if you possibly can help her. If she is seeking financial grants or yearning for media coverage, perhaps you can provide her with some contacts. In other words, don't fight her; join her.

3. If you are a male and consider yourself power-motivated like the college vice president in our case study, you might look into your own attitude toward women administrators. According to Dr. David G. Winter, professor of psychology at Wesleyan University, "men who desire power generally don't get along very well with women, tend to be divorced, have many lovers and their partners appear to be less happy."[15] If you fit the picture, find a male boss.

4. When your superior excludes you from meetings that you feel you should attend, plan a strategy that will convince her why you should be present. Write a proposal that stresses the advan-

tages and skills that you can bring to the discussion. Do not—and I emphasize this—do not list for her the benefits *you* will gain from attending. She's not interested in advancing your education. She wants the status of being Chief Power Broker. Moreover, she's watching the bottom line—what it will cost the company in time and dollars for you to be out of the office. Your conversation might sound like this:

Manager: I don't believe it is necessary for you to fly to Atlanta to outline your project plans to the Southern Group. I can spell out your ideas for them, and if they have any questions, they can call here and you can elaborate.

You: I think I could get a better handle on what they want if I met with them in person. It would save us money in the long run. Then I wouldn't have to revise any of the initial plans I drew up. I'm also thinking of the vice president's time; he'll have to schedule a number of meetings with me to transmit their ideas for the project. It is probably more cost-effective if I can sit with the Southern Group and work it out right from the start.

Are you fascinated by the idea of learning how to play the power game? Then don't hesitate to copy or imitate successful aspects of your administrator's management style. There is always something we can learn from others. As author Edward de Bono says, "We can learn lessons; we can gain new perspectives; we can learn what works for them and what does and does not work for us; we can learn what to focus upon; we can learn broad strategies that do not rely for their efficiency upon our role model's personal style."[16]

A Woman in Power

Gazing upward, the four-story brownstone looks like all of its neighbors—baroque, a little nondescript, and a shade forbidding to those standing on the quiet side street in Manhattan. The limousine that was sent to get me coasts noiselessly to the front steps of the house. Kathleen, the thirty-nine-year-old president of one of the largest perfume companies in the world, steps off the curb to offer me her hand in greeting.

Inside the brownstone, a museumlike interior surrounds us—original oil paintings by Titian and Rubens, ancient Chinese vases, and primitive African figures. Kathleen lives here with her lover, an art collector and scion of one of New York's wealthiest families. Dressed in a tangerine wool suit, with custom-designed jewelry at her throat and wrist, Kathleen's outfit and high heels make her seem even taller than her well-documented six feet, an asset for anyone in power.

She gives the impression of immense energy. Only her green eyes with the strange flecks of gold gaze quietly at me. Dozens of miniature bottles of expensive perfumes are backlighted in a special display case in a far corner of the room. On top of the case, her friend's priceless collection of pre-Columbian figures stares belligerently down at this modern depravity. Kathleen follows my eyes, and a mischievous smile crosses her face. "No, the perfume bottles aren't part of the decorator's scheme—he thought they were hideous. But they're my talismen—lined up to remind me of how I got here from the Back Bay of Boston."

It Began with Irish Stew

"I'm interested in your rise to the top and how you handle the power that is inherent in your position," I ask. "Don't worry about taking notes," she says, "it's not a rags-to-riches story. More like an Irish-stew-to-paté-de-foie-gras tale of the kid who grew up among Boston politicians and saw what power meant. My father was an attorney who loved politics—dabbled in local stuff all his life. He used to tell me, 'Kathy, remember, the only thing that matters is power.'

"I forgot his advice for a while; then I recalled his words after I took a bachelor's degree in chemistry and found a part-time job that paid me practically nothing. I was experimenting with ingredients to make the perfect cologne—the last word in sexual allure—when I realized I couldn't market it without a degree in business. The rest of the story you probably know—an M.B.A. from Columbia, thirteen years of hard work, plus a mentor. A wonderful man who believed in my talents."

Termed the "ultimate power broker" last year by a respected business columnist, Kathleen says labels don't bother her. "No one is opposed to power except those who don't have it, but want it.

"I consciously study the symbols of power and the characteristics of powerful people," she admits. "I've learned to look and act as though I have power. This started long ago, even when I didn't possess any real power."

She says she mastered yoga so that she could control her body with her mind, appearing calm and in command at all times. "I totally reject that 'dress for success' idiocy of the late seventies and instead dress for dramatic impact. To be visible. No one ever ignores me when I walk into a meeting. I practice flaring my nostrils in front of a mirror and lifting my head like a champion stallion. Silly? Possibly. But these are the gestures and controlled facial expressions of the powerful men I used to meet in Dad's office back in Boston."

Power Is Like Sex

The lure of money is not what drives Kathleen. She says it would be foolishness on her part to believe wealth is unimportant; but it doesn't exhilarate her like the act of exercising power. "Power to me is as much a turn-on as sex. I get a charge from outwitting a business opponent. I like to hand out special favors to those more powerful than I. Nothing thrills me more than having someone at the top of a big corporation owe me a favor. I love the fact that I was invited to join an exclusive committee of several hundred of the most powerful women in the country. Perhaps you're not aware of it, but your company must meet certain standards for you even to be eligible."

Kathleen says that as she rose to the presidency of her company, she occasionally used a temper tantrum to get her way. "No more. I'm beyond that now. But if you want to be known as a power figure, you must be flamboyant—consciously display your power."

Is she a manipulator? "Absolutely," says Kathleen. "I enjoy making deals and being on the winning side. I also have learned to hire the most talented people in their field—the hell with yes-men or yes-women. I like ambitious, creative employees who want personal success."

"What advice would you give a young man or woman who truly craves power?" I ask.

Kathleen glances briefly at the perfume display in the corner and says quietly, "Look as though you own the company, and eventually you will. Cultivate the physical signs of power. Dress for it. Speak as though you have it. Associate as much as possible with those in power, and never, never be ashamed of wanting it."

Power Game Strategies for the New Manager

The option of being a power broker is available to few women in the nation. Why? Because corporate America is virtually all male. Although women fill almost a third of all management positions, the majority are mired in the middle ranks, possessing little or no policy-making authority. Of 1,362 top executives surveyed last year by Korn/Ferry International, only two percent were women. Says Richard M. Ferry, president of the California-headquartered executive search firm, "the pressure is off of us to hire women in senior executive positions. We have to work two or three times harder to locate them. Why should the client have to pay for this extra effort? Am I going to be a crusader to force them to?"[17]

With this harsh reality, your opportunities to wield true power in the workplace—if you are a woman—are slim. However, whether you are male or female, if you receive a promotion, you're going to have to learn some of the subtler moves of the power game in order to hold your position. Even if you don't enjoy the struggle for power or the rewards it brings, you should master a few of the strategies that will help you be an effective power player.

1. If you are a woman and have an ambivalent idea about success and power, work to overcome it. Remember, you deserve what you can achieve.

2. Don't be ruthless in your striving for power. You can be bold, self-confident, and authoritative, but you don't have to tramp on others to attain your goals.

3. Plan a life outside of the office, so that if your power game fails, you don't end up bitter over your sacrifice. According to investment banker Heather Evans, "When virtually one's whole life is work, unhappiness at work creates an insidious psychological trap."[18]

4. "When you gain power," Dr. Rebecca Stafford, president of Chatham College, says, "become confident that you can wield it graciously." She adds, "Sit lightly in the seat of power. Remember, you are the king and you can afford to be kind to those around you."[19]

5. "I advise women aiming for leadership positions to develop *very* thick skin," advises San Francisco Mayor Dianne Feinstein. "You have to be resilient and prepared for the fact that you will win some and lose some. Stamina is critical!"[20]

6. Accept the fact that your next-level managers are going to be less willing to help you advance as the pyramid narrows toward the top. Understand that they too crave power; then you will be happier and freer to plan your own strategies, and they will be based on reality.

7. Role play to gain power. If you behave as if you have it, people will believe you do.

Diane Posnak, vice president of Handy Associates, maintains, "Success begets success! If you act as if you have power; look as though you have power—you will have power." She adds these tips: "Dress well—expensively, if possible; become visible in the media; make sure your office is reflective of your power; establish control in meetings; and keep people waiting a reasonable length of time when you have an appointment scheduled. Role playing will help you gain power in the workplace."[21]

Boss Assessment Questionnaire: The Woman Power Broker

Evaluate your boss for the power broker management style with the following rating scale:

A—Always or yes	5 points for each A answer
S—Sometimes or occasionally	3 points for each S answer
R—Rarely or never	1 point for each R answer

1. Does she apparently enjoy the amount of power that she has? ______
2. Does she perceive her own interests as more important than those of your organization? ______
3. Is she creative in her approach to her job rather than rigid and unbending? ______
4. Does she like getting her own way rather than giving in to someone else? ______
5. If she has to make salary cutbacks, does she make certain that she is not one of those whose income is diminished? ______
6. Does she seem to enjoy being the martyr for her job—refusing to take time off; cutting short her vacations; taking work home in her briefcase; claiming her health is being affected by the stress at work (but never doing

anything to help herself); maintaining that no one realizes how much she worries about the company? ______

7. Does she complain about the enormity of her job and the sacrifices it entails, telling those who competed for it, "It's not worth it" but at the same time reveling in the power she has? ______

8. Does she like to have under her control vast amounts of information about the company—its employees, its policies, its quarterly reports, its annual reports, its profit and loss statements, and its weekly and monthly sales figures? ______

   Says Michael Korda, "Controlling information has an advantage as a game of power. It tends to make the person who controls it seem indispensable—and the indispensable game, though risky in the long run, is an excellent secondary move in acquiring and holding power."[22]

9. Does her office reflect her need for power in its location, in its proximity to the chief executive officer of the organization, in its view, or in its access to the top person either through a private door, hallway, or a special elevator? ______

10. Has she marked the inviolate space within her office with a personal symbol such as a paperweight on her desk, perhaps given to her as a gift when she received a sought-after promotion; a picture of her prize-winning Hereford bull; a distorted purple ceramic ashtray made by her son in third grade; color shots of her and her lover on the ski slopes of Switzerland; or a certificate of course completion from the American Psychological Association? ______

Most of these objects are trivial and meaningless to someone else, but to the power broker they are "power-site markers," just as important to her as a fire hydrant is to a male dog.

11. Has your boss attempted to stake out as much physical territory as possible, taking over space that no one else has any use for and that apparently isn't necessary for the daily operation of her division? ______

    This could be any type of space, ranging from the master file rooms to the video screening areas. Power equates with having a variety of operations under your aegis, all of which are located in areas other than your office. Even though you might have no immediate need for the business centered in those spaces, the mere fact they are a part of your division gives you increased power.

12. Does your boss prefer to conduct important business, necessary for the ongoing operation of the organization, at fixed meetings? ______

    I am not referring to the casual fifteen-minute strategy session that is held informally during the workday, but rather to the board meeting or executive committee meeting that is vital for the continuation of the company. According to Michael Korda, "Fixed meetings automatically become invested with magic significance. It is not necessary that such meetings be productive, or even that substantive questions be discussed; it is only necessary for them to take place."[23]

Total Score ______

60–45 You have a highly power-oriented boss.
44–29 Your power broker boss should be your role model!
28–12 Your manager must be unique. She apparently does not crave power. Perhaps you should think of going after her job!

Chapter 4

When You Have an Intimidating Boss

The Queen Bee Syndrome

Selene strides into her "early-American-look" dining room with a warm smile and two steaming cups of coffee. "Okay," she says, "I promised to tell you about my supervisor, The Great Intimidator. Where shall I start?"

I can't help but admire this youthful-looking "reentry" woman of forty-two who carved out a successful real estate career for herself in six short years. Always the quintessential homemaker, with two sons off on their own in distant cities, Selene says she "became bored with kaffee klatches" and started selling houses because it looked easy. Her selection of a midlife career has paid off. "I've won trips to Tahiti and Hawaii as 'salesman of the month,' " she reveals, "but I'm not a five-million-dollar pitchman yet! Give me time; there are still a few big ranch-styles out there just waiting for the right buyers. I'm going to find them, too."

As we sip our coffee and add on a few extra pounds with Selene's strawberry cheesecake—delicious testimony to her culinary talents—she says, "If only you could see my boss. It's like looking at the Statue of Liberty. She's tall, fiftyish, heavy. Everyone who works for her is intimidated by her size—an impenetrable force—and she knows the value of her appearance in making the rest of us feel six inches high. Imagine huge, chunky jewelry, big gold chains around her neck, like a wine steward weighed down with keys to the wine cellar. You feel her presence whether she's in the office or not. When she writes us memos, it's always with a heavy black felt-tip pen. That makes a statement, you know! Am I intimidated? You bet, and so are the other fourteen men and women who work for her."

Selene says her manager's formidable appearance is a perfect introduction to her office demeanor, which earned her the dubious title, The Great Intimidator. She sits behind a massive desk and appears to hold court, presiding from what subordinates call "the throne"—an extra-tall, heavily upholstered swivel chair. When she hands out new listings, the silence is audible. No one raises a question for fear they might antagonize her and trigger one of her legendary temper tantrums.

Selene's boss is definitely what Susan Easton calls "the Queen Bee, the rare woman in management who succeeded long before the feminist movement arrived."[1] If you are a young woman just starting your career, be wary of this type of older boss, for she feels that her success has been earned at great personal sacrifice—which usually is true. Her attitude is "I did it on my own, so you can, too." She tends to resent the advantages that have opened up to women in their twenties and thirties, and seldom will she extend a helping hand.

"When our boss offers some aid to one of us, we become very wary," says Selene. "This is because her assistance is contingent upon a favor in return. Quite often, this means taking the blame for something she has done that isn't in the best interests of the company. For instance, she decided that our sales staff should cover two additional areas of new housing developments. We're understaffed now, so it was impossible to broaden our territory. But we tried, and it failed. While we bombed in selling the houses in that project, everything else slipped. We were so busy, we couldn't take proper care of our original territory. Sales went way down.

"You would imagine that my boss would admit, 'It was my responsibility. I took on more than we could handle.' On the contrary—she intimidated all of us into taking the blame for what was her error in judgment. The head of the real estate conglomerate called each of us into his office—individually—to give us a pep talk on 'standing up on our own two feet and selling hard.' Do you think that one of us had the nerve to say, 'It wasn't my fault—my boss had the great idea for expansion?' Hell no. We all took the shit and agreed that we weren't trying hard enough. Now, who says we aren't intimidated by our office manager?"

A Positive Response to Bullying

Blaming a subordinate for one's own mistakes is a reprehensible act in the workplace, no matter who does it. But when it happens, it's your responsibility to try to understand why your boss is bullying you and how you can best overcome your own feeling of helplessness. Some time ago, a friend of mine took her sense of inadequacy and turned it into an effective response to her boss's intimidation. She had a hunch that her supervisor felt overwhelmed by her job and was taking it out on her employees in various ways—like forcing them to work during their coffee breaks, or ordering them to stay overtime without additional pay. So my friend approached her and, in a friendly, cooperative way, said, "I know we have a pile-up of incomplete projects. Perhaps I can stick around for a few evenings and assist you in getting them moving." To her astonishment, the boss became absolutely enthusiastic, suggested that my friend join her for a "quick bite" after everyone had left the office, and then said that they would work together. With communication thus established, the two women began functioning as a team, and the result was a promotion and a salary raise for my clever pal within six months.

As you can see from this story, the tendency to become bogged down on the job—or, as in the case of Selene's boss, to deny responsibility—sometimes is a result of an intimidating manager's efforts to make sure that no one trespasses on her turf or that she never looks bad to the higher-ups. Insecure and often threatened by younger subordinates, she is terrified that employees' mistakes will reflect poorly on her and that top management will discover her failings.

Says author Betty Harragan, "Women who are fighting to hold their place must be especially vigilant. They must keep watch every moment because their tenuous hold will be threatened from two directions: more proficient players will try to fool them, assuming they are amateurs in rules; and violations will be penalized more harshly for women than men."[2]

How to Use Your Boss as a Resource

Pete, a quiet, unassuming man of twenty-five, works for the same manager as Selene, but he has put all of his efforts into developing his boss as a major resource for himself. Do you think that this means he is unaware of her intimidating tactics? Absolutely not! But he is working around them and succeeding. He tells me that even in college he was certain of his goals: "I wanted to own the biggest real estate office in the city by the time I was forty. This meant going to work at the most respected firm in the area or the one with the largest volume of sales. I found both requisites in this company, and frankly I intend to learn all I can before I leave."

During his first week on the job, Pete says that he "knocked heads" with his boss almost immediately. "I was new . . . naive . . . and damned inexperienced. I told her I had a problem . . . a customer who was pretty dissatisfied because I hadn't sold his house, even though I had been pushing it for two months. I barely got the words out of my mouth when she butts in and says in a bellow that could be heard all over the place: 'What did you do wrong? Overprice it? Show where the roof leaks?' I was immediately on the defensive. I found myself stuttering . . . explaining that I wasn't at fault . . . the owner was to blame. I had told him what the house would bring. He insisted that he wanted twenty-five thousand more. 'It's a crazy price, I know,' I told my boss. "But what am I gonna do? He's the seller—I'm just the schmo trying to shove it on to some poor sucker."

Pete says his boss ignored him after her initial outburst, told him it was his problem and if he couldn't solve it, he was in the wrong business. He adds, "From that moment on, I knew the score . . . and maybe, I grew up a bit, too. I decided to learn all I could about selling houses and property. The people involved . . . the office politics and why my boss hassled all of us the way she did." He gives me a wide grin and an "A-okay" sign with his thumb and forefinger. "Since our conversation, it's been a piece of cake," he says. "I've become friends with my boss, and I really think she's going to help me when I'm ready to move up. She doesn't know how to create the best job climate for the people who work for her, but she sure knows the real estate business."

Tactics to Know Your Boss

Learning what made his boss tick represented a major breakthrough in Pete's work strategy. Before he understood the motives behind her often negative actions in the office, he could never cope over the long term; moreover, he would continue to be foiled in all his efforts to gain advancement. You might find useful some of the following tactics that Pete used to develop his manager as a valuable resource, despite her intimidating management style:

1. Show genuine interest in the scope of your manager's duties. The more you find out about her higher-level functions, the better you will understand the operations of the entire company.

2. Attempt to gain her confidence so that you are aware of how she perceives the duties of her subordinates in relation to her own functions. Are you necessary in her eyes, or are you in a "throwaway" position?

3. Ascertain your manager's relationship to her own boss. Is she using an intimidating way of supervising because she herself

is treated this way by her supervisor? Does her boss put undue pressure on her? What does he think of her?

4. Find out whether your boss is viewed as an executive on the fast track. If she is, and if she is known to be very difficult and demanding, your peers and upper-management colleagues will admire you for your ability to get along with her. You will also be seen as a person who is chugging right along with a winner.

Pete is shrewd, and he's going to make it in business. He realizes that his boss, despite her intimidating style of management, is going to be the single most influential factor in this particular phase of his career. You don't work in a vacuum in an organization. You are dependent—all the time—on others to help you get ahead. And your boss, whether good or bad, will have a significant influence on your upward mobility. In addition, those with whom you work, as well as the culture of the company, will help shape your responses to your workplace. George deMare, author and business communicator, says,

> You may be a fine worker, skillful in your job, your intentions may be the best, your integrity and character first rate, but if you do not know how to get along with others, how to understand and relate to the organization, its beliefs, traditions, ways of doing things, its morals, its manners, the things it will tolerate and the things it will not, its policies and most of all the kind of people it cherishes and requires, you will not last long.[3]

Adapt to All Managerial Styles

How important it is for all of us to relate well to each other in the workplace was pointed up to me recently in a conversation that I had with Jimmy Jones, vice president for employee relations for the Gannett Corporation. A famed defensive end for the New York Jets in the late sixties and early seventies, he now reports to Madelyn Jennings, senior vice president for personnel at the same corporation. Mr. Jones says, "I come from a sports background where I'm used to head-to-head confrontation. When things don't go the way you want, you don't just roll over and play dead. However, in the business world, when a decision is made and you don't have your way, then it's time to play the team role. All is forgiven, and you go along with your boss and those you work with."[4]

Mr. Jones's belief in the necessity for learning to adapt to all types of managerial styles was echoed by his superior, Madelyn Jennings. Charged with directing the "people program" of Gannett Corporation, involving 32,000 employees, she says with a smile, "When Jimmy and I walk into a room filled with people who don't know us, some might wonder who the 'black' and the 'broad' are. What they don't realize is that we represent the changing workforce of the eighties and that we are a highly respected team in our industry. Sure, we bump heads, but we have enormous respect for each other. I, too, was a competitive athlete—a real plus factor—for it puts us both in a position where neither of us can intimidate the other. Another point for a good workplace relationship is when the manager and her subordinate have a mutuality of commitment to the company. Both of us feel this way about Gannett; so the corporation's concerns do come ahead of our own."[5]

Office Gossip is a No-No

Sometimes, intimidation by a boss takes the form of cajolery. Employees are coaxed into confiding their co-workers' most intimate secrets to a prying manager. Karen, a recent college graduate who works for a woman supervisor in a graphics firm, was flattered by her manager's invitation to lunch, and she felt obliged to answer her friendly questioning about other employees. The young woman opened up with an avalanche of gossipy tidbits and unconfirmed stories about a man who headed another division in the same company. Shortly after that fateful lunch, the male boss was abruptly told his services were no longer needed.

His department then was consolidated under Karen's boss, who had earlier been so charming over chicken salad and sherbet. Could this have been coincidence? "Absolutely not!" says Karen, unhappily aware of her part in his dismissal. "I was overwhelmed by my boss singling me out for special attention. . . . I sort of felt I owed her something. So I passed on office gossip that should have been filed under 'trash.' "

In the case studies that you have just read, I hope you realize that none of the employees who report to a boss with an intimidating management style has given up. Each one still is learning by trial and error how to adapt to her manager's sometimes unorthodox ways. Selene admits that she attempts to stay out of The Great Intimidator's office whenever she can; Karen says she has learned to keep her mouth shut about the personal lives of her co-workers; and Pete has earned the title of Wunderkind in his office, for he has developed a series of strategies for coexisting happily with his intimidating boss. You might want to consider his ideas:

1. Be straightforward in all of your dealings with your boss. Just because she sometimes acts in a bullying way doesn't mean that you should be dishonest or devious in order to avoid a possible encounter with her.
2. Stay out of her way as much as possible.
3. Never, never confide in her, for she might use your tale of woe against you.
4. If she is bullying one of your peers, attempt to discreetly play the mediator and smooth things over.
5. Don't put on a "meek mouse" act, but at the same time avoid a confrontation with her if you can.
6. And most important, don't discuss your weaknesses with her, for she'll never let you forget them and will continually use them to further intimidate you.

The last strategy is very critical in dealing with this type of manager, for even though you might correct your perceived weaknesses and add to your knowledge with daily experience and extra study, she will always remember your initial discussion. For years afterward, you might find that true confession aimed at your jugular.

When Your Furniture Wanders Off

Management by intimidation is recognized as one of the least productive supervisory methods. Yet in my interviews with subordinates, it emerges as one of the most widely identified styles used by some women bosses to exercise authority. An unpleasant outcome of the process of socialization that women have experienced—the development from child to adult—in a value system that emphasizes male superiority, this way of managing devalues subordinates and builds up a false sense of power in the female manager.

Don discovered his new supervisor's craving for power when he entered his office one morning at a small bank in Seattle. He found it strangely empty, as if he had moved out. The twenty-four-year-old loan officer says, "I couldn't believe it. My easy chair was gone. So were the lamps and a small table. Nothing was left but my desk and an old straight-backed chair. I didn't know what had happened. . . . All I was worried about was a meeting I had scheduled with two local businessmen that afternoon. Where on earth were they going to sit?"

As far as Don's new boss, Marian, was concerned, his guests could sit on the floor. She had joined the institution only ten days before as senior loan officer, and the bank had not supplied her quickly enough with office furnishings to match her new title. She is Don's superior, and she was using a form of organizational bluffing to make her point. She felt she had to intimidate someone—and fast. Unable to strike back at the administrative hierarchy, she targeted Don and asked the maintenance men to raid her unwary subordinate's modestly decorated office. As an executive once told me, "Even though I don't give a tinker's damn for an oriental rug or a Nakashima chair in my office, all that expensive furniture makes a statement. You're either a big deal or a little squirt in the organization, depending upon how important your suite looks and how close it is to the ultimate seat of power."

Bluffing is Intimidation

Don's boss was right in her desire to have an impressive office, but she went about fulfilling her wish in the wrong way. She shouldn't have waited over a week to show her displeasure with the negligence of the banking institution. She also didn't have to vent her wrath on her mild-mannered, innocent subordinate. What she should have done was to scream bloody murder on her first day there, when she discovered her new office was as bare as the late Yul Brynner's skull. She should then have hightailed it to the bank president's undoubtedly palatial quarters and asked for a few minutes of his time. List in hand, she could have impressed upon him the necessity for her to have an important-looking office quickly in order to influence the proper people—*proper* meaning those local entrepreneurs looking for venture capital to start high-tech enterprises that would generate need for more capital. She could have demanded a conference table, easy chairs, an extra phone, a sofa. The works. And what ever else it takes to bolster her image in front of the institution's clients.

Don's initial reaction to his denuded office was anger and bewilderment. Then the stubbornness of his Irish grandfather came to the fore, and his carrot-top hair bristled. He became one persistent employee. In a 007 maneuver after hours, he rounded up the same maintenance men and lugged the abducted furniture from his manager's office back to its familiar place in Don's cubicle. He had to repeat the performance twice before his new boss got the message. The ridiculous cops-and-robbers drama ended when she came to his door several days later and meekly asked if she could "please borrow" a few chairs and a lamp until the bank furnished her office. Her bluff had failed.

Bluffing as a form of intimidation is a normal practice in organizations, and as Albert Z. Carr says,

> The ethics of business are not necessarily those of society, but are rather those of a poker game. In both games the ultimate victory requires intimate knowledge of the rules, insight into the psychology of the other player, a bold front, a considerable amount of self-discipline, and the ability to respond swiftly and effectively to opportunities provided by chance.[6]

Carr doesn't see these ethics as dishonest, but as merely a "special" brand, applicable in business as well as in poker.

Don's response to his female manager's intimidation, although a bit unorthodox, was successful. The most obvious coping strategy for this common type of situation is to confront the supervisor who has lifted the goodies from your office and resolve the problem quickly. Twice during my years as a subordinate, I was the victim of "chairnapping"—big, squishy, comfortable chairs that my managers coveted. The crime is not a female aberration; once it was my male superior at a university, and another time it was my woman boss at a publishing house. In each instance, I was very open and forthright: "I see my favorite chair has taken a stroll down the hall. When you finish your nap, may I please have it returned?" Needless to say, on both occasions the itinerant furniture was back in my office the next day, and I felt victorious, having successfully countered an intimidating action.

When Your Boss Lacks Self-Esteem

People who feel psychologically powerless often try to intimidate their subordinates in a neurotic attempt to dominate and exhibit control over others. Such managers must always be right, and they cannot tolerate disagreement. According to psychotherapist Rollo May,

> Some degree of power in the sense of mastery and control over one's fate is necessary for feelings of self-esteem and well-being. When a person's exercise of power is thwarted or blocked, when people are rendered powerless in the larger arena, they may tend

> to concentrate their power needs on those over whom they have even a modicum of authority. . . . In other words, people respond to the restrictiveness of their own situation by behaving restrictively toward others.[7]

Whatever the motive behind the intimidating management style of your boss, it is up to you to determine how to handle the inevitable conflict that results. And that isn't all bad. Conflict, as you know, is inherent in any workplace, and it is vital that you learn to live with it. It can result from a situation as innocuous as having your office moved farther from the seat of power, or it can be the aggravation you experience when your boss intimidates you into working the entire weekend. Whatever the problem, you must cultivate a mental attitude by which you can say to yourself, "I'm okay, no matter what. I can handle this management style without any long term damage to my own sense of self-worth."

How Nurses Boss Future Doctors

One segment of the workplace in which subordinate men and women face unexpected intimidation is in the large teaching hospitals—generally affiliated with a university—where medical students and interns threaten nurses right on their own turf. In territory that has been theirs since the days of Florence Nightingale, nurses retain through intimidation their managerial superiority over the future doctors for approximately two to three years. Then, in an extraordinary role reversal, following their graduation and year of residency, the new physicians become the authority figures to whom nurses must defer. At this point, everyone is insecure. Nurses see their new bosses as still wet behind the ears and lacking hands-on experience. The freshly minted M.D.s revel in the role reversal, but are terrified of the responsibilities accompanying the title Doctor. Is it any wonder that conflict ensues between the two groups and that intimidation is rampant on both sides?

Ed, a fourth-year medical student at Johns Hopkins, says of his experience with an intimidating nurse, "I became violently ill when I saw my first intestinal operation. The OR nurse standing beside me didn't offer any help; all she said was, 'What's wrong, kid? Did you choose the wrong profession? Maybe you had better be a truck driver instead of a doctor.' The problem is, I had been thinking that myself before she said it. Man, did I feel like a nerd! Especially when I realized that I expected the nurse to be supportive because she was a female."

One of Ed's male classmates sauntered over to us as he was telling me this. "You'll forgive me, but I couldn't help overhearing your conversation. Let me tell you my story. Just last week in the intensive care unit, I felt myself blacking out. . . . The sight of the tubes poking out of every part of the patients' bodies; the fact that not one of those people in the beds could say a word—they were all on ventilators—my own feeling of helplessness. Here I am a doctor, and there wasn't a damned thing I could do to make them feel better. And all I wanted to do was sleep—I had been up for forty-eight hours straight—so I began to sway, fighting not to pass out. One of the ICU nurses noticed me and said contemptuously, 'You look a little green. If you're such a baby, you had better step in the hall and get some air. I don't give a damn if you want to faint, but you had better not fall on one of my patients!' "

If You Need to Cope with a Nurse

Fortunately, if you happen to be a nurse or medical student locked into this unique interaction, take heart, for the situation is self-limiting. In about three years the parameters of authority will be clearly defined, and you will be either one or the other: the physician/boss or the nurse/subordinate. At this juncture, most nurses accept the inevitable and will take orders from the doctor-in-charge, no matter the gender. Coping strategies for this sometimes convoluted relationship are limited. However, you might find that the following ideas will ease your migraine if you are a medical student or a new resident reporting to a woman nurse:

1. Recognize that you're going to make mistakes, possibly quite a few over the next few years. But relax—you will not be directly responsible for the patient's well-being for a long time.
2. Defer to the nurse who is working with you. Chances are good that she is thoroughly professional and has been in the health field for many years.
3. Take responsibility for your successes or failures. You are in a learning situation, where everyone will be critical of you, so don't be defensive.
4. Keep healthy. Medicine is an exhausting profession, both physically and emotionally. If you take care of yourself, you're going to be better able to cope with any intimidation you encounter.
5. Be open-minded. Your nurse-superior will be able to teach you a great deal that you didn't find in textbooks. So listen carefully and in a respectful way. You might be surprised at what you learn.
6. This is one workplace situation where you shouldn't take the initiative. You are dealing with human beings, where a wrong move can be disturbing, if not damaging. Check with your superior before assuming any authority.
7. Set priorities so that when you are under intense stress, you can complete your duties in an orderly manner.

Interacting with Your Manager for Your Benefit

Last year, a longtime friend of mine told me about the management training seminar that her company had sent her to for an intensive six-week program. She said, "I was amazed at the huge sum of money our corporation spent on teaching us how to be 'decent human beings.'. . . Basically, I found that the whole goal of their training program was to help people get along better with each other."

In a few simple sentences, my friend verbalized what many experts say about effective management styles: that the group of skills taught by human relations experts, career counselors, and management consultants all have one specific purpose—to teach us how to interact with each other with understanding, compassion, and respect. The boss who manages by intimidation diminishes you as a person, not because this is her aim, but rather because she feels insecure in her own job.

Anticipate Conflict to Avoid It

A bullying managerial style is never effective between boss and subordinate, but it is particularly destructive when it involves a woman manager and women under her aegis. It tends to reinforce the feeling of helplessness that so many subordinate women bring into the workplace, and it calls forth in the minds of uninvolved employees all of the negative stereotypes of women bosses that have been prevalent in our society for far too long. In dealing with an intimidating management style, it is most important for you to learn to anticipate when and where conflict is most likely to arise. Try to avert the crisis, if possible, and resist the urge to answer back.

Coping strategies are not easy. And the reason is simple. Your manager's behavior stems from many complicated causes, among them her upbringing, her need for ego gratification, her fear of her male boss, her superambition, and her insecurity. It is impossible for you to probe the reasons for her behavioral style: all you can do is learn how to cope.

I would prefer to see you try to handle this situation rather than seek other employment. Why? Because at some point in your career, you will once again be faced with a manager who supervises in an intimidating manner, and you might not be able to run as easily the second time around. Be a risk-taker. Stay! And select your strategy from among the following options:

1. Make a mental truce with your manager, and resolve to do the very best that you can on the job. Don't permit that bully-

ing managerial style to detour you on your career route. This is only one obstacle; there will be be many, many others ahead of you.

2. Take a good, hard look at your body language when you are working together with your manager. Are you giving out signals of despair or vulnerability? If so, make a resolution, right now, to change. Points to watch:

- Posture: Relax. Don't fidget. Act confident. Use large body movements in conversation. Keep your shoulders and arms loose.
- Eye Contact: Don't look at the ground when speaking to your manager. Make eye contact, and speak directly to her in conversation.
- Voice: Make a conscious effort to change your vocal quality if you have a high-pitched, squeaky voice. (Practice in front of a mirror at home). A voice in the lower registers commands more attention and gives you more authority.
- Conversation: Don't be submissive, apologetic, or tentative in your professional dealings with your boss. You will command more respect if you display positive attitudes in a good strong voice and deliver your message in a confident, forceful style.

3. Don't be defensive if your effectiveness on the job is under evaluation. We all can learn a great deal from objective recommendations—even when management's style is overly intimidating.

4. Don't concern yourself with your manager not liking you. Her intimidating way of supervising has nothing to do with you personally. Moreover, it's time you grew up. Not everyone you meet will like you. You're going to aggravate some people, and there will be others who exasperate you. Just remember—you're not in a popularity contest. You just want to learn to get along with others in a positive way.

5. Try to learn as much as possible about the business you are

in. Knowledge is power, and your manager's coercive behavior will be much less threatening if she knows that she needs your expertise.

6. Try to find a mentor within your company to offset the negative effects of your manager's actions. It is possible that this person will ultimately help you on to the next rung of the success ladder.

7. Learn the difference between aggressiveness and assertiveness. Then try some of the latter on your boss. You just might shock her into some positive management strategies.

8. Practice tolerance when you are aware that the intimidating style of your boss is affecting you. Remember, she was one of the pioneers in reaching a management level in a male-dominated workplace. It isn't easy!

9. Put more effort into developing the potential in your job. Remember Jonathan Livingston Seagull in Richard Bach's best seller of the same name? You, too, can pursue higher goals as Jonathan did, and then you might discover that the sky is the limit and that the lack of people skills shown by your boss is really unimportant in your flight to success.

A Boss Who Prides Herself on Intimidation

As I walk down the cool, dim hall to the penthouse apartment, I see the door is ajar, held by a deferential gentleman who acts as chauffeur, butler, and houseman to Monique, the well-known founder and president of a home for handicapped children. He gives me a welcoming nod and ushers me in to the bright, glass-walled sunroom where his chic boss is putting the finishing touches on a breakfast table so lavish that it would make an ideal center spread for a home and garden magazine. Monique greets me with a hug and pulls out a green-cushioned wrought-iron chair. "Before we get down to the business of interviewing," she says, "please try one of these croissants—I baked them just for you. My family brought the recipe with them when they left Paris in the sixties." I nibble the delicate roll—its flaky texture reminds me of a pastry shop on the Bois de Boulogne. Monique says wistfully, "That's one fast-food item I have never become accustomed to in America—those hideous croissants and so-called French pastries in the shopping malls. *Merde!* They're not fit to eat."

"You promised to tell me," I remind her, "why you feel that your reputation as an intimidating manager is well earned and why it doesn't disturb you."

She breaks in. "Not in the least. It is necessary to act this way sometimes to accomplish what you believe in. And I'm proud of what I've done. I'll go into the reasons, but before I do that, I must let you know, I was curious about the word *intimidate*. So I looked it up in the thesaurus. Do you know what some of the synonyms are? *Bluster, browbeat, bully, ruffle, badger, wheedle*—and a few more I can't remember. Such words don't worry me, for I've had to act out every one of them to support my special project—a home for handicapped children. And as you know, I am still 'intimidating' the whole damned city for a cause that I think justifies my actions."

A handsome woman with elusive charm, she is equally at ease soothing the aches of a crippled child and asking for monies in the austere offices of a foundation president. Monique is married to a wealthy congressman. They have one child, a twelve-year-old son with cerebral palsy. An influential member of several hospital boards and a political activist, she made a decision over ten years ago to devote every spare minute of her time to founding a home for children with severe handicaps. She's the first to tell you that she took on an impossible task when she resigned from the hospital boards to become president of the new organization.

Making People Feel Guilty is an Art

"Let's be realistic. Few people are interested in a child with Down's syndrome or cerebral palsy until it hits home. I wasn't any different. When Dickie was born handicapped, I became active in the group known as Parents Against Defects. Till then, I always had let someone else worry about crippled children."

Monique describes her many years of fund-raising for the home—first to obtain the land, then to get the structure built. "To be honest, I try to make the people I approach feel a little guilty about refusing me money for such a heartwarming organization. I wheedle funds from those whom I know, and I plead for money from those whom I don't know. I cover every angle—foundations, private philanthropists, grants, medical endowments. Sure, I ruffle plenty of feathers along the way—all the time—but you have to be tough, and sometimes intimidating, if you want both your employees and the public to support something you believe in."

Acquaintances of Monique say she is fortunate, for she is the wife of a popular politician. Her marriage, according to these people, opens doors to her that would otherwise be closed. She is always able to persuade her wide circle of friends—with a little arm-twisting, they claim—to give money to the children's home. "And never forget," one added, "it's all tax deductible."

Monique says she now has a paid staff of about twenty—"I used to be a one-man operation"—with fifty volunteers available for special occasions. She explains, "I know our organization better than anyone else, so naturally I expect everything done my way. I can't be bothered teaching, and I haven't time to argue. Basically, my subordinates haven't the ability to make important decisions; when they try, they usually get the instructions backward. For this reason, I tell them to bring everything to me for a final check—even if it means waiting in line for approval. And yes, I do expect total loyalty and dedication. When I must be here until eleven at night, I fully anticipate that my staff will stay late as well."

Although I find it difficult to delve for more information, I feel it's necessary to be blunt in order to get Monique to reveal her management philosophy. She had told me before our meeting to "be brutally open" with questions. She added, "This is the only way I can offer meaningful help to employees with a woman manager as dedicated to a cause as I am."

I plunge in. "What about your reputation for screaming at your subordinates and embarrassing them in the office?"

She is amused. "Don't you scream at your children sometimes? After I reprimand my employees, it's all forgotten. They know I love them, and I never ask anything of them that I wouldn't do myself. When they're ill, I'm the first one to take care of them."

I feel another tough question is in order. "One of your subordinates said she has 'terrible guilt feelings' if she has a bad back or a cold and wants to take a day off, for you seem to expect each employee to come in no matter what. Aren't there legitimate reasons for occasionally staying home from the office?" I ask.

Monique bites her lower lip, obviously perturbed by my probing. "Yes," she finally answers, "but in an office like ours, where we are seriously understaffed and overworked, a subordinate should stay home only under the gravest circumstances—a death in the family or a critical illness. Otherwise, I expect everyone to be there on time each day. After all, I come in with a cold—even with pneumonia—so a few sniffles or a sore back is no excuse to stay away from the office."

Throughout our conversation, one point becomes overwhelmingly evident. Monique, the manager, is utterly dedicated to her charitable undertaking. Moreover, she is willing to sacrifice anything and to intimidate anyone in order to guarantee the success of the home for handicapped children. The turnover in her staff is unbelievable, according to the board of trustees; yet Monique's motives for her actions are justifiable in her own eyes.

If You Intimidate, Try to Change Your Style

Women managers who direct nonprofit organizations like chamber music groups, art centers, symphonies, dance groups, operas, or, as in Monique's case, a facility for handicapped children, often assume an intimidating supervisory style. Wheedling and threats are part of their managerial repertoire; the negotiations and delegation tactics of the business world seldom are used.

Their singleminded focus on the success of their organization becomes an obsession. This can lead a woman manager to attempt to play bossy mother all her life, badgering the men and women who work for her in the manner described by Sey Chassler, former editor-in-chief of *Redbook*: "In business neither female nor male Wendys work out well—there is, after all, no place for hovering parents in business, because business is not a family, it's a team."[8]

You may recognize some of your own managerial actions in Monique's attitudes and actions. If you do, and you don't want to be known as a person who blusters and browbeats her subordinates and peers, you could experiment with a fresh approach to management. These strategies will help you attain your goals while retaining a competent staff:

1. Stop acting maternally and reprimanding your subordinates with loud deprecations and screams of disapproval in front of everyone. This creates tension and stress and earns you a reputation as a bullying boss.
2. Try to train some of your subordinates to take over a few of your responsibilities. As your organization grows, you will not be able to do everything yourself. When you find that you can't, you will become a browbeater. Avoid this by preparing your subordinates for different roles according to their abilities.
3. Don't expect everything to be done exactly your way in the office. You must allow your employees what management expert Peter F. Drucker terms "the option of learning through doing and self-development through practice."[9]
4. Delegate to your subordinates different facets of the job to be accomplished. If you feel confident in their abilities, you will be less inclined to intimidate them with threats of what will happen if they don't produce. As author Nathaniel Stewart explains, "Growth breeds growth. . . . Each achievement, goal attained, successful program and break-through nourishes all contributors: subordinates, managers and the company."[10]
5. After you delegate a task, try not to interfere. You must allow your subordinates the option to fail. Only by an occasional failure do we learn.

6. Don't bully your subordinates into staying late when you do. In normal situations, this isn't necessary, and the urgency probably exists only in your mind. Save this type of request for a crisis circumstance.

7. When your employees must stay late to complete a job, reward them. This should be an exciting reward, not just a sandwich and soft drink. Take all of them to a good restaurant or to a dinner theater. In this way, you demonstrate that you value them and their dedication to the organization.

8. Don't forget to praise, rather than intimidate the persons on your staff. Kay Cushing, senior vice president of Ketchum Public Relations, says, "A marvelous rule for a manager—male or female—is when you find someone doing something right, tell them so! Offer them genuine praise; don't ever overpraise."[11]

Boss Assessment Questionnaire: The Great Intimidator

Evaluate your boss for an intimidating management style with the following rating scale:

A—Always or yes	5 points for each A answer
S—Sometimes or occasionally	3 points for each S answer
R—Rarely or never	1 point for each R answer

1. Does your supervisor ever threaten her subordinates in order to force them into her desired mode of behavior? ______
2. When your boss discovers an incident of poor or inadequate performance by a man or woman who reports to her, does she raise her voice and embarrass that person in front of co-workers? ______
3. Is your manager the last person in the office to find out if someone who reports to her has serious problems at home, like a sick child or a financial crisis? ______

4. Does your boss bring her own personal problems to the office and let them affect her so that she intimidates her subordinates by being overbearing? ______

5. When you or one of your peers go to your boss for assistance and she's in a tense, deadline situation, does she ever lose her temper and blast you out of the office? ______

6. Are you uncomfortable about expressing your ideas concerning work projects to your manager? ______

7. When a project doesn't go well, have you found that your boss tends to "slip out from under" and blame the poor results on the rest of you? ______

8. If your boss wants a project completed ahead of schedule, does she use all types of coercive tactics to get you to meet her arbitrary objectives? ______

9. Have you found that your manager "borrows" your creative ideas or those of your peers and then brings them to the attention of the president of the company as her own brilliant suggestions? ______

10. When your boss wants to know something about the private lives of your colleagues, does she tend to badger you or your co-workers into revealing something that you know should be kept confidential? ______

11. Does your manager constantly remind you and your co-workers that whatever performance evaluations she turns in on you can make or break your careers? ______

12. Does your manager use various symbols of her power to intimidate you? ______

These could include: an office decorated to the nines while you slave away in a monastic cell; small at-home parties for her office pets (you're not one); frequent vacations while the rest of you pant in a 90-degree heat wave; expensive designer clothes that make you feel like Orphan Annie before she met Daddy Warbucks; or a "closed door" policy so that you feel totally out of the decision-making process.

Total Score ______

60–45 Your boss is a fearsome intimidator.

44–29 You are fortunate—your supervisor has some intimidating qualities, but she is bearable.

28–12 Your boss is confident and secure. She does not need to use intimidation to be an effective manager.

Chapter 5

Missing: The Ability to Negotiate

Emotional Confrontations

Conciliation. Compromise. Mediation. These are just a few of the human relations techniques that you must rely on if you report to a woman boss who lacks the ability to negotiate effectively. Female managers who have this trouble see every problem in the workplace as a black or white situation, with no gray areas for bargaining or maneuvering. "They often personalize the negotiation conflict," says Dr. Margaret Neale of the University of Arizona, "rather than viewing it as an example of the way the system works."[1] Basing their interactions with you on this kind of perception, women supervisors sometimes approach each issue that must be resolved with their subordinates as an emotional confrontation.

Pearl is exhausted from this type of session with her boss when I meet her at her apartment in Greenwich Village. A television writer for a popular daytime "soap," she had said she was having a difficult time with the woman she reported to, a senior writer who refused to participate in any negotiations with her on the scripts they both had to produce for the series. Sipping white wine, with her long legs tucked under her on a velvet-covered chaise longue, Pearl looks vulnerable, more like an innocent teenager than a woman who has spent eight years in the TV jungle of cancellations, reruns, and aborted series.

She says, "Last week I put together some new story lines for our fall television program because we had lost so many of the original cast. It was hellish! One of the male leads had to be written out, for he had found a job off-Broadway . . . the mother-in-law from the series had to be shipped someplace for a prolonged visit because in real life she had developed phlebitis in one leg . . . our romantic lead is pregnant and showing . . . and the producer wants his brother to have a walk-on role. That might be possible, but the brother hasn't acted since he was the pumpkin in a second-grade production of *Cinderella*. Jeez, do I have problems!

"Anyway, I try to work them out and hand in the script concept to my boss. She in turn is expected to do her version of the series, and then we negotiate the manner in which our ideas are combined. Even though we have differing opinions, we're supposed to be unified by the time we submit the final script to the head of our writing team.

"But it never happens like that! The process breaks down when I deliver my script to the senior writer. She criticizes the story line, drags her feet on which characters should be knocked off, changes the love interests, and inevitably ends up competing with me for the final version of the series. I don't mind the criticism—there has to be a healthy give-and-take of ideas—but I do resent her unwillingness to negotiate the finished series.

"We're the first two women to become members of a writing team for the afternoon 'soaps,' so for that reason alone, we should support each other and come to an agreement. This field has been a male bailiwick practically since the invention of television, and the men still aren't exactly putting out the welcome mat for us. You know the old bullshit—'women don't belong here'—well, my boss is well aware of this bias, so all she has to do is meet me halfway and say, 'I'll do two scripts; you write two.' Or, 'I'll concentrate on the openings—you focus on the closings.' Or whatever. Instead, she scribbles me little notes about her position and remains adamant, not budging an inch. I just don't understand her attitude, because I know she needs me."

Recognize Your Need for the Other Party

Professor Earl Brooks of the S.C. Johnson Graduate School of Management at Cornell University, a nationally recognized expert on negotiations, says, "Most people believe that women are better negotiators with men than with other women. I find that when women bargain with each other, they tend to be more competitive. In negotiating, the important point to remember is to recognize your need for the other party. When you fail to do that, you have problems."[2]

In the case of the two script writers, Pearl's boss is forgetting the basic, underlying philosophy of negotiating success—everyone wins something. Although she recognizes the importance of having her subordinate as a collaborator for the TV series, the senior writer has not acknowledged her need for the subordinate's contribution to the joint effort. Moreover, it is generally impossible to negotiate without a face-to-face meeting to resolve the difficulties. Scribbling notes to your opponent is counterproductive. A successful negotiation, according to author Gerard I. Nierenberg, includes "a knowledge of human nature, preparation, strategy—all combining to satisfy needs."[3]

A middle-management woman working for a large twenty-four-hour supermarket chain in Manhattan is approached on a busy Saturday afternoon by one of her subordinates, a young assistant manager from the produce department. The employee says to her boss, "I need a transfer to the night shift as soon as possible—like the end of this week." Her manager glances up from the accounts she is working on and asks sharply, "Something wrong? You're doing a great job—the fruit display has never looked better." The subordinate looks down at the floor and mumbles, "I know. But my husband just got a promotion to night supervisor at his plant, and he wants us to have the days together."

The woman manager is tired and irritated. All she can see is another problem on a busy weekend. "Well, you've put me in a fine position," she says. "Thanksgiving is coming, and we'll be jammed with customers all day long. I need your experience to handle the produce turnover—to check that the fruits and vegetables are displayed properly and that the potato and onion bins are kept filled. You can't do this to me now."

Obviously agitated by her boss's response, the subordinate doggedly pursues her point of view. "I understand your problem, but I have to think of my marriage. I'm even willing to give up being assistant manager of produce if you'll let me work the night shift."

At this point, the manager wipes the ink from her leaking ballpoint pen, looks up in anger, and replies, "No, I'm sorry. You're just going to have to stay where you are. I need you in that job, particularly at this time of year. Tell your husband to take up a hobby or to start jogging."

The manager is nonplussed when her subordinate turns away and says, "I quit as of tomorrow. It isn't worth it to me to ruin my marriage."

Here, as in the case with the senior script writer and her subordinate, you can see why you must always have a personal strategy for any negotiation with your boss—particularly, say some experts, with a woman boss. Dr. Blair Sheppard, assistant professor and director of the Human Resource Management Center at the Fuqua School of Business of Duke University, says, "My clinical observation is that although women are perceived as more likely to negotiate a solution where they satisfy both sides, they are less likely than men to interpret something as a negotiable item."[4]

Plan Your Personal Negotiating Strategy

How, then, do you shape your own personalized negotiation plan so that you feel confident of bargaining productively with your woman boss? Culled from more than a dozen "building blocks" for personal negotiation strategies devised by Dr. Earl Brooks[5], I feel that you might find the following suggestions helpful:

1. In all your negotiations, expect that you will win something and lose something. In the words of an old song, "You've gotta give a little." Dr. Brooks says, "You can't be stiff-necked, arbitrary, sanctimoniously right, or rigid in negotiating with others."

2. Directives and orders will not lead to mutual agreement. When your boss has the power to punish you or to withhold something you want, you aren't in any position to give her orders. Just make up your mind that you're willing to deal.

3. Look to the long term, even as you deal with the immediate issues in negotiating with your boss. If you plan on staying with your company for years to come, both of you should emerge from the negotiation as winners. In this way, your workplace relationship will remain friendly and mutually beneficial.

4. Remember that you and your manager have objectives that are both in common and in conflict. In the supermarket confrontation, the assistant produce manager needed the job—but under a different set of conditions. Her boss needed her, but she built failure into the relationship when she refused to discuss the issue or to make a different arrangement. Unity between the two became impossible, even though they had the common goal of retaining the subordinate's job.

5. As a follow-through to Rule 4, it is important to remember that in the negotiation process, you and your boss are interdependent. It's vital that whether you're a low-level subordinate or a middle manager, you size up who needs whom before you start making demands. As Dr. Brooks puts it, "Often negotiation reverses traditional authority relationships, for the parties need each other at different levels."

When You Want a Raise

On the other side of the country, far from the produce section of that Manhattan supermarket and the sudsy soap operas of the

TV studio, twenty-nine-year-old John is attempting to negotiate a raise with his boss, Betty Ann. Both work for a moderate-size research and development company in Palo Alto, California. A skilled programmer, John is enrolled in a graduate program at night at a nearby university. He envisions a challenging career for himself in the computer industry. He's happy with his job, he finds Silicon Valley an exciting place to be, and he's dating an aspiring actress who is assistant stage manager at a theater in San Francisco. "Free tickets," he tells me with a wink, "but no free lunches."

But John's taste probably wouldn't be satisfied with a Coke and a burger, even if they were thrown in with the tickets. He prefers four-star restaurants and Pierre Cardin suits—an impossible dream on his present salary. For this reason, he's asked for a meeting with his boss. The conversation goes something like this:

John: I think you're pretty happy with the job I'm doing, and frankly I'm enjoying it tremendously. I like the chance to think for myself and to see the end results of my work.

Boss: That's wonderful—we're quite pleased with you. I'm sure that you have a future with our company. But it's obvious that something is bothering you.

John: You're right, Betty Ann. I feel I deserve to get a raise, because I'm doing most of Bill's work since he left the research lab. Also, my own department has expanded, so I now have three people reporting to me.

Boss: We've been aware of your situation, John, and maybe it *is* time for a promotion and salary hike. But as you know, things are tight, and you do receive great benefits from the company—health and accident insurance, pensions, and your four-week vacation in July.

John: Well, I'll tell you, I want the raise so much—not only because of my added responsibilities, but because inflation has decreased the buying power of my salary to the point where I'm behind on my car payments—that I'm willing to take just two weeks vacation and work three hours each

Saturday if you can find it possible to give me a raise and some stock options.

Boss: Sounds fair, John. Let me figure out how much the company can afford, and I'll get you that extra bit in your paycheck as soon as possible. I'll give you an amended contract this afternoon.

Don't Forget the Perks

So far in his negotiating, John has done well; however, now that he has his manager at the point of making him an offer, he must take the process one step further. He has to discover how much she is willing to give him in exchange for his suggested compromise. You have been in this position many times, I am certain. And you were a little afraid of being a tough negotiator, right? That's the response of most of us. You know the feeling—"I've shoved this far, I better not try for any more. Just might lose everything." You're wrong. You have to find out what you're going to receive, such as perks, stock, or another form of equity; when the raise becomes effective—for instance, this month or next; and how much.

I rather like Mark McCormack's idea of "negotiating backward." Named not too long ago by *Sports Illustrated* as "the most powerful man in sports," a business consultant to more than fifty of the Fortune 500 companies, Mr. McCormack says, "I find it helpful to try to figure out in advance where the other person would like to end up—at what point he will do the deal and still feel like he's coming away with something. This is different from 'how far will he go?' A lot of times you can push someone to the wall, and you'll still reach an agreement, but his resentment will come back to haunt you in a million ways."[6] In other words, negotiate so that you and your manager both benefit from the agreement, with no ill feelings on either side.

Negotiating, considered by many psychologists to be an element of human behavior, is simple by definition, but infinitely broad in scope. Gerard Nierenberg, president of The Negotiation

Institute, says, "Every desire that demands satisfaction—and every need to be met—is at least potentially an occasion for people to initiate the negotiation process. Whenever people exchange ideas with the intention of changing relationships, whenever they confer for agreement, they are negotiating."[7]

John and his boss, Betty Ann, are excellent examples of two people striving for a goal from which they both benefit. They did this simply, without angering each other and as a cooperative venture. You will notice that they came to terms over John's salary hike by his clever emphasis on issues they could agree upon—John working extra hours each Saturday and giving up two weeks of his month-long vacation. Neither he nor his boss dwelled on the point of difference—a raise—when the company could ill afford it. Their common interest level, which gave impetus to the negotiations, was that John continue his fine work for the company. He and his boss showed good faith in this cooperative approach—often a more satisfying way to bargain than in a highly competitive manner.

If you are in a situation similar to John's, in which you know you deserve a raise but your company is in a tight financial bind, try giving up something in return for the extra dollars in your paycheck. Author Edward de Bono claims that "a good tactician in negotiation is aware that he may have to retreat at times." In fact, he adds, "The idea of giving away something in order to achieve something much more important is one of the basic rules."[8]

Women Bosses Are Sensitive to Personal Cues

As you can guess from these very different examples, the negotiation process takes many forms. Whether they are gender-specific has never been proved to everyone's satisfaction. A prodigious assortment of contradictory findings relating sex to negotiation behavior does not really give us any definitive clues as to whether men and women differ greatly in their ability to bargain cooperatively with one another.

Only one research finding seems to emerge as important to our discussion of your negotiating with your woman boss, and that is that women appear to be more sensitive than men to a number of interpersonal cues.[9] It is wise for you to bear this in mind when you are bargaining with your female boss, for she will be on the lookout for a variety of signals to strengthen her arguments and to provide leverage for her position.

If you want to use winning tactics and come away with the best of the bargain—a formidable feat when you're the subordinate—show by your behavior that you understand personal cues affecting the negotiating process. You should be aware of the value of:

1. Nonverbal Communication. Appear calm and possessed when you negotiate with your boss. Don't shift your feet continually, and don't clasp and unclasp your hands. Make direct eye contact with your manager and hold it—no one wants to bargain with a shifty-eyed person. Research has shown that about sixty-five percent of our understanding of a two-person conversation comes from the nonverbal rather than the spoken word.[10]

2. Silence. You can learn a great deal by saying nothing and urging your manager to talk freely. Most people are fearful of keeping too quiet. But in negotiating, silent watchfulness can pay dividends.

3. Your Timing. If the subordinate in the produce department of the supermarket had timed her request better, she might have negotiated an agreement with her boss. If you'll recall, she approached her manager in the middle of a busy Saturday afternoon before Thanksgiving—the worst time to "talk turkey."

4. The Setting. In most cases, subordinates must do their negotiating in their manager's office—not exactly neutral ground for employees to feel at ease. However, if you possibly can switch the bargaining meeting to a coffee shop or a private corner of the company cafeteria, you might be more comfortable. Try to avoid negotiating when your boss is taking a break, rushing to a meeting, or heading for the ladies' room. When she's concerned about puffing up her hairstyle, your negotiation just might fall flat.

5. Punctuality. When you are involved in a positional bar-

gaining situation, it pays to be on time. Nothing will put your boss in a worse mood than standing around for fifteen minutes waiting for you to appear. In very few cases, she might appreciate your late arrival and use it to catch up on her correspondence. Tardiness, however, is a big gamble, and you should be aware of its possible negative effects on the negotiations.

6. Listening Carefully. Most of us use the interim when the other person is speaking to plan our answers or rebuttal to their premise. Don't do it! Concentrate. Evaluate what your boss is really saying, mentally review what she has told you, and file away some of her key points for further negotiation. Above all, don't fake the listening process in front of a woman manager. Remember the researchers' conclusions—women are more sensitive to personal cues than men!

Your Negotiating Isn't on Track

If you are willing to negotiate, but your boss prefers to dominate, you might find the technique of "negative inquiry" an excellent strategy for putting your negotiations on track. Elaina Zuker, an organizational consultant and author, explains: "Negative inquiry is a useful technique for getting your critic to open up and to state clearly what his or her objection is. By not becoming defensive, by simply probing and asking more and more questions, you are eliciting information that can be valuable to you in your future dealings with your boss. Once you have heard your critic out . . . you are ready to negotiate."[11]

Be a Detective

Let's assume that you feel it's time for you to receive a promotion. After all, you have been with your company for three years; you believe that you have done a good job, for your colleagues compliment you on your talents. But you have a boss like the senior script writer to whom Pearl reports. She isn't very skilled at negotiating; she seldom opens up and states her position; and you know from past experience that if you press too hard for a compromise on an issue, she will want to be the winner. At this point, it's up to you to assume the role of detective and ask questions so that you can understand the mental processes of your boss. It's the only way to get negotiations rolling. Your negative inquiry might go like this:

You: I've been thinking lately—it's been over three years since I came to work here, and my job title and responsibilities are pretty much the same as at the beginning. Perhaps I ought to ask for a promotion.

Boss: Sounds like a good idea. Why don't you?

You: I guess I have been afraid. But, okay. Am I going to get a promotion soon?

Boss: Probably not for a while. I don't think you're ready.

You: Why not? Are there problems?

Boss: For one thing, you're trying to do everything yourself. That was the reason I gave you an assistant—so you could delegate more and start learning to be a manager. I feel that delegation is one of the critical skills you need in order to be promoted. In addition, you had better work on your decision making. You have to be more positive and not change your mind a half dozen times.

You: I didn't realize you felt this way. I thought that the more work I turned out, the happier you would be. I presumed you wanted my talents rather than those of my assistant. As for changing my mind all the time—you're right. I'll have to watch that.

Boss: I'm glad you understand my viewpoint. I was a bit hesitant about bringing up these shortcomings—afraid you would misunderstand.

You: On the contrary, I'm appreciative. Now I know where I stand, and I can do something about my problems. May I approach you about the promotion in about four months?

Boss: Absolutely. You should have cleaned up your act by that time, and we'll have something to talk about.

You Can Get What You Want

In this relatively simple dialogue, you and your boss have opened up a whole world of communication—the first step in profitable negotiation. You have not acted defensive, and you have not lost your own sense of self-worth. You have merely applied some creative techniques to recognizing the desires of your woman boss. With this type of feedback, you're going to be able to negotiate with her in the very near future.

Almost any topic that invites some type of disagreement can evolve into a negotiation issue—even in an esoteric professional field like dress designing. Onile, a lithe black artist with the high cheekbones and satiny caramel skin of her Tahitian forebears, works in the garment industry of Los Angeles, designing high-fashion sportswear. She recently joined a new company as head designer—a challenge that at first thrilled her but that now has become a source of stress and frustration. Why? Because for the first time in her eleven years as an artist, she has to seriously negotiate in her professional life in order to maintain her creative integrity.

"When I reported directly to the male president in the last company," she says, "I never had a problem getting approval for my designs. It wasn't that he was particularly easy to please, but he never demanded outright that I change a certain pattern or color interrelation. Generally, he would say he felt a little unsure about a particular design and ask 'What if?' . . . I would weigh his suggestion, offer another option, make a few concessions, and we were off and running. We both gave a little, so each of us ended up pleased.

"For the past four months, since I took a more prestigious, better-paying job, it's a whole different ball game. My immediate boss is a middle-aged woman merchandiser. We have very serious disagreements over my designs—some are so bitter that I think we could use an arbitration expert to settle things."

"Why? Is it because men are more accustomed to negotiating?" I ask.

Onile thinks about my question for a moment and then says, "There are several factors involved here. Perhaps some ageism, a little racism, and undoubtedly jealousy. Even though she is my direct boss, she had no input into my being hired. So that bothers her. When I first came, she initially tried to establish dominance over me by calling me honey or dear. I hate that maternal, patronizing approach—it's a total putdown—as well as a white-over-black statement.

"When I brought out sketches for our new line recently, everything came to a head. She ordered me to redo my designs exactly as she wants. 'Your concept is all wrong, my dear. You have no feel for what is needed in the marketplace.' Shit! As the young black employee, am I supposed to back off and concede easily? No discussion? No negotiating over the final product? That's not me. I'm willing to go halfway, but I'm not about to bastardize my art completely for her whims. She has to give in some, too."

When an Ultimatum Works

The week after I spoke to Onile, she became so angry and distraught over her inability to negotiate with her new woman boss that she sent an ultimatum to the president of the company. He was in Paris for the spring fashion shows. In the telex, she threatened to break her contract unless she could report directly to him or to his vice president for merchandising. The president didn't want to lose Onile's creative potential, so he wired back a simple three word reply: "It's a deal."

If the executive had not valued his employee's talents quite so much, he could just as easily have sent back a shorter reply: "You're fired." The dress designer had not acted properly in going over her manager's head, and she deserved to be reprimanded at the very least. Rather than react in anger to the merchandiser's criticism of her art, she should have attempted to mollify her woman boss until the president of the firm returned.

One valid way to do this, according to top negotiator Mark McCormack, is to acknowledge your boss's feelings. "This is the oldest psychological technique in the world and works just as well in negotiations as it does in any other form of human relations. It sounds as though you have accepted or committed to something, when in truth all you have 'accepted' is how the other party feels."[12]

Although the conflict is not finally resolved in this way, employees who have used a conjunctive clause on their boss claim that they can turn almost any bitter negotiation into an all-around back-slapping, congratulatory get-together. The magic phrases to tell your woman manager that you understand her feelings are: "I know just how you react, but . . ."; "I understand exactly what you mean, but . . ."; "I couldn't agree with you more, but . . ."; and "Yes, but you know how it is. . . ."

With a sympathetic acknowledgment of her manager's position, Onile could have used a variety of negotiating techniques to keep the relationship from disintegrating any further. One of the best approaches is to be candid and honest. You actually disarm your boss by admitting "This is very important to me" or "I don't want to lose this account. Couldn't we cooperate on seeing it through?" When you try this approach, you'll find that both you and your manager regain your perspective and anger evaporates.

We Negotiate Every Day

You, like everyone else who reads this book, have been in not one but hundreds of situations where negotiation was the only solution to your problem. Stop and think for a moment how the necessity to negotiate touches your life virtually every day. You need a loan for your house, but the interest rates at your bank are too high. The engine in your car dies two days after the one-year warranty expires, and you frantically contact the dealer. You want a plum assignment in your office, but the boss could decide to give it to one of your four peers. For any one of these daily frustrations, your choices are narrow. You could give in and forget about what could have been; you could bully the other party—a bit risky when it's your boss—hoping to "win"; or you could negotiate a settlement that is satisfactory to both you and the supervisor with whom you are dealing.

To my way of thinking, negotiation is one of the most important skills you must master in order to gain management success. As we become increasingly dependent on the role of the computer in our society, negotiation expert Gerard Nierenberg says, "the role of the human negotiator grows in importance."[13]

Had Onile, in our case study, been a little more skilled in effective negotiating, the situation with her woman boss probably would not have ended in a dramatic showdown. Her reckless bravado in going directly to the top—or at least over the seas—to contact her president with a "take it or leave it" challenge could have ended her career with that company. Fortunately, Onile's artistic genius convinced the chief executive to bypass her manager and keep her on. But she made a formidable enemy in the woman merchandiser by confusing negotiating with machismo. And she lost the chance to develop a personal strategy for negotiation that would have stood her in good stead all her life.

Try Prenegotiation Tactics

If you are in a situation where you feel that your manager's attitudes about your race, age, or appearance have an adverse impact on your ability to negotiate with her, take these major steps in prenegotiation tactics:

1. Recognize that your boss could have a point of view of prejudice about your race, religion, politics, or physical appearance that will start you both off on the wrong foot from your first day on the job. You can argue, rationalize, or agonize, but you're not going to alter her thinking. What you have to do is confront the issue.

In a virtually all-white professional field like dress design, to be black, exotic, and talented is apparently not the ideal combination for Onile to impress her woman boss. What she has to do is to set the stage for her on-the-job negotiations by confronting the issues of her race and youth head-on with her biased supervisor. If you'll recall, to be a Catholic running for President in 1960 also brought to the fore many prejudices that John F. Kennedy dealt with openly at the start of his campaign. By attacking the topic of prejudice with candor, he cleared the air for a discussion of national issues.

2. Don't hide your real feelings about your manager's attitude. If you conceal your hurt over the way you are treated, you are not able to negotiate from a position of confidence and strength. When you feel this passive and beaten down, run—don't walk—to the nearest assertiveness training class.

3. If you are disturbed by the way your woman boss addresses you—"my dear," "honey"—tell her so! What you view as demeaning or as a putdown, your manager actually might see as a kindness.

4. Before you begin negotiating, put yourself in your manager's shoes and become aware of her feelings. What prerogatives of hers are being threatened by your needs? What is there about your goals that she resents? Onile's boss in our case study is worried about her image in the fashion world if she makes a wrong call on the artist's preliminary designs. In addition, if the designs aren't appropriate for the new season and don't sell, she will be at fault when her company loses money. As an uncreative, middle-aged woman (if she were creative, she would be the designer), she probably feels some jealousy for the youthful good looks and artistic talent of her employee.

Can Negotiating Be Taught?

Can negotiating skills be taught? "No question about it," says Dr. Margaret Neale. "I believe that all of the negotiating skills are trainable, and because women pick up on social nuances much more readily than males, eventually, with experience, they should be excellent negotiators. Right now, they have to learn a couple of things. They must begin to view most commercial exchanges and social contracts as forms of negotiation. They have to understand that the majority of transactional processes can be negotiating processes.

"For instance, the first day's assignment for my classes is to bring in an object—toothpaste, shampoo—and give me proof that they negotiated for it in the transaction. The men will come in triumphant with one rose or a six-pack of beer—each item negotiated for successfully. They enjoy the bargaining process. The women often are a bit embarrassed, less creative, and not exhilarated. They negotiated for the object, not because it was an exciting game, but because the instructor had given them an assignment. Men tend to like the ego-building facet of negotiation and the sense of mastery and control that it gives them."[14]

Dr. Roy Lewicki, associate dean of graduate business programs at Ohio State University, corroborates this perception of women's attitudes toward negotiation. "Their style of bargaining and their attitudes toward the process are derived from female upbringing in managing conflict. Strategies of accommodation and avoidance of conflict cannot lead them to a win/win solution. How well they do in negotiating is determined by how willing they are to take a stand, to endure some pressure, and to defend what they believe in. Frankly, if males were brought up in the same noncompetitive environment that females traditionally were reared in, men would have similar problems in negotiating. And I'm sure that some do."[15]

Strategies to Overcome the Fear of Negotiating

If you are aware that your upbringing has had some impact on your ability to bargain capably with your boss, here are some additional strategies that should help make you less hesitant in getting started negotiating:

1. Take a Dale Carnegie course or a specialized seminar in assertiveness training so that you can overcome your timidity and embarrassment about being a bargainer.

2. Don't worry if your boss is a friend and you need to negotiate. As Roger Fisher and William Urey of the Harvard Negotiation Project say, "Pursuing a soft and friendly form of positional bargaining makes you vulnerable to someone who plays a hard game of positional bargaining."[16] If you are more concerned with building and maintaining your friendship with your manager than with obtaining a raise or an extra week of vacation, then take the soft approach. The catch is, your boss might be playing hardball.

3. Control your own temper if your boss has an emotional outburst. Emotional reactions sometimes can push negotiations along, but they're risky, for they can lead to violent quarrels. You might suggest to your manager that a rule is adopted that only one of you can show anger at a time. This can put some humor in a tense situation and save face for both of you in the bargaining session.

4. If you are hesitant to challenge your boss in negotiation because you perceive the process as beneath you or as indicative of a "fishwife" tendency to "haggle," just watch the news media carefully for a few days. You will find that top leaders of the world participate in negotiations almost every minute of the day! Moreover, they enjoy the feeling of power that comes from a win/win situation in which they perceive themselves as the victor or the worthy loser.

5. Plunge into negotiations with your woman supervisor as if you had been doing it all your life! According to Benjamin Fischer, director of the Center for Labor Studies at Carnegie-Mellon University, "the way to become a skilled negotiator is to negotiate. The more experience you get in bargaining, the more adept you

will become. I don't know if you realize that negotiators in major labor disputes are not professional negotiators."[17]

Negotiating Often Begins in the Kitchen

"I'm great at calling in the chits, and that translates into negotiating," says Barbara, director of educational programs for a Fortune 500 corporation. "Women managers don't realize that they learned how to negotiate at their mother's knee. She would say, 'Honey, go borrow a cup of sugar from the next-door neighbor and tell her that she can have in return the two cups of flour that she said she needs to bake her cookies.' And away the little girl would go to bargain for her mother—never realizing that she had participated in a winning deal that made both neighbors happy."

We're in Barbara's art deco office, with its brilliant primary colors and angular furniture, part of a renovation project in the corporation. "Behavioral psychologists suggested the 'happy' decor to lure us into work every morning," explains Barbara with an impish twinkle in her eyes. "But it sure didn't work for my subordinate, Pete. He used to be the most sullen, disgruntled, unhappy individual on earth until I learned how to negotiate with him."

Barbara said the problem started when she was appointed to head the educational department, and her employee was already in place, hired by the former manager—a white male. "From day one of our relationship, Pete showed me no respect; in fact, he was insulting. He also was nasty, flip, and undependable. I gave him the ball and told him, 'Run.' He either avoided doing his job or sneered at me when he was in the office. The whole situation became impossible. I was living on Valium to calm my nerves. Then I remembered Mom negotiating with the principal to get me out of school early for a Christmas holiday; bargaining with the owner of the corner grocery to lower his prices to compete with the big market in town. I decided it was time to transfer her housewife tactics to my fancy office."

Grabbing her youthful subordinate on one of his rare appearances in the department, Barbara invited him out for a beer. At the corner bistro, Pete opened up to her plea of "Let's negotiate some sort of compromise—we can't go on this way."

To make a long story short, says Barbara, "I asked him bluntly, 'Am I giving off the wrong signals?' Then he opened up. Pete told me he had never worked for a woman boss—let alone a *black* woman boss. He was embarrassed—felt less a man—also felt very isolated for, at that time, he was my only subordinate. So my color only exacerbated an already bad situation. Our ages had something to do with it, too. He was about twenty-four and I was five years older, so he resented taking orders from a female contemporary.

"After we talked the whole mess out, everything came up roses. We negotiated a deal that left us both feeling like winners. Among other things, he promised to be pleasant and give our relationship a chance. He also vowed to be in on time and to carry his load of the work. I gave him the two afternoons he wanted off to attend some judo classes (which I never knew about), and he offered to work two evenings to make up the time. I made the package so sweet that he couldn't help but come around. We became a team, and I volunteered to be his mentor. When I was promoted, I recommended Pete for my job. Best of all, when he and his wife had their first child—you-know-who was the godmother!"

If the Situation is Untenable, Negotiate

This true success story points up the value of negotiation. Barbara came up with her own strategies for a win/win ending that focused on rewards that she could offer as the boss. Notice what you can learn from her skilled negotiating:

1. If you are a middle manager having problems with a subordinate, bring them out in the open—preferably away from the

office and in pleasant, nonthreatening surroundings. Relax with your employee and *communicate*.

2. Listen carefully to your employee's gripes: then give him or her your perspective—honestly.

3. Find out what your subordinate wants and needs.

4. Offer your own concessions that will let you both achieve a desired goal. Use persuasion where necessary.

5. Don't worry if, after a short period of time, a glitch appears. It is natural in any negotiating that there will be a hitch or setback. Treat the temporary lapse as a minor problem that needs an additional resolution—and solve it.

6. Let your subordinate know—with praise, monetary rewards, or additional responsibility—that the negotiation has produced the desired results.

Boss Assessment Questionnaire: The Ineffective Negotiator

Evaluate your boss for her ability to negotiate effectively with the following rating scale:

A—Always or yes	5 points for each A answer
S—Sometimes or occasionally	3 points for each S answer
R—Rarely or never	1 point for each R answer

1. Instead of negotiating in order to reach a mutually advantageous agreement for the two of you, is she more likely to turn the bargaining process into a contest of egos? _____

2. Is she concerned more with saving face for herself than with resolving the thorny problem between you? _____

3. When you finish negotiating with your manager, do her bargaining skills leave you with an uneasy feeling that you were "taken"? _____

4. When she enters into the bargaining process with you, does she pretend to have the authority to negotiate, when in reality the responsibility for negotiating rests completely with the compensation department or the human resources division of your company? ______

5. When you are negotiating with her, does she ever use subtle gestures or cues to let you know who really has the power in your bargaining session? ______

6. Is your boss apt to hold back important concessions and agreements with you until the last possible moment, figuring that she can win more by having you sweat it out and then cave in out of fear or frustration? ______

7. Does your boss have a reputation—or perhaps a track record—for trying to stonewall her subordinates in a negotiation? ______

8. Does she avoid the obvious alternative methods of resolving an issue so that the negotiation is beneficial to the two of you? ______

9. Is your boss afraid to say no and therefore may renege on a negotiated agreement with you after all the issues have been settled? ______

10. Does she appear to lack confidence in her own ability to negotiate and thus will try to avoid the process at all costs? ______

    Many women managers are afraid of failing, particularly with a male subordinate who is a skillful bargainer; therefore, they will give in immediately to outrageous demands.

11. Do you find that negotiating creative problem solving is impossible with your woman boss because she is what author Herb Cohen calls "an emotional or visceral adversary"? ______

According to negotiation expert Cohen, a visceral opponent not only disagrees with your point of view but disagrees with you as a human being. He says, "Your boss may even attribute sinister or nefarious motives to the position you espouse." When your supervisor is an "emotional enemy," he adds, she contributes to "a climate of inordinate stress where judgments are formed, accusations may be made, and scorekeeping takes place."[18]

12. Does your boss try to avoid negotiating whenever possible because she views the entire process as beneath her—a form of haggling that a lower-class individual might undertake in a flea market, bargain basement, or outdoor bazaar? ______

Total Score ______

60–45 Forget a win/win outcome; your boss cannot negotiate.
44–29 Your boss probably negotiates effectively approximately fifty percent of the time.
28–12 Celebrate! You have a boss with negotiating skills.

Chapter 6

The Nondelegating Female Boss

When Your Manager Welcomes "Overload"

The citizens of a small town outside of Newark are in a state of panic. A tank car carrying hazardous chemicals from an adjoining state has jumped the track and spilled its cargo containing high levels of PCBs—a chemical suspected of causing cancer—near a heavily populated area. Alerted by the news media to the possible danger, the mayor of the town declares a state of emergency until special precautions can be taken to assure the safety of the townsfolk. According to the mayor's office, evacuation is being contemplated.

At a chemical spills cleanup company just ten miles away from the accident, Dr. Karen Lundquist, a nationally respected environmental toxicologist, strides over to one of her most talented subordinates. "Jack, there's a spill of PCBs on the east side of town. Let's head out and see what's going on."

With a burst of nervous energy, her energetic staff member springs from his chair, sending reports, books, and pens flying off his cluttered desk. "Sounds great, boss lady. You want me to hotfoot it over and tell everybody to keep their cool until we assess how bad the situation is?"

"No," replies his boss. "I want to go with you: they'll probably need my experience."

The young scientist's pleasant features cloud over. He drops his kidding demeanor. "But, Karen, hold it. I feel quite capable of handling the problem—after all, I wrote my doctoral dissertation on the handling of PCB spills. I've been involved with you on a dozen emergencies like this over the past three years, and you're already overloaded with four other hazardous waste accidents. How much can one person handle?"

Jack's manager is slipping into her coat as she responds. "You just don't understand, Jack. There are some things that I don't feel I can delegate to anyone—no matter how capable the person is. I also like keeping busy every minute and making all the decisions. That's no reflection on your skills. I know how good you are."

The blond toxicologist whisks through the door. Her subordinate hastily grabs his coat to follow her to the parking lot. His jaw is set in a look of resignation. He has gone through the same scene a hundred times since he accepted the position under Karen.

Delegation Is Difficult for Everyone

This is a classic case of a manager who needs to know more about one of contemporary management's most important but least understood functions—effective delegation of work. Virtually anyone you speak to in the business world believes unequivocally in the principle of delegation. But according to Dr. Peter F. Drucker, "Delegation comes extremely hard to most managers." One of the nation's foremost specialists on effective management and the author of a half dozen seminal books on the topic, Dr. Drucker adds with a touch of whimsy, "I'm the world's worst delegator myself—I even insist on answering my own telephone in the office."[1]

The most common mistake that managers make, he says, "is

thinking that they're supposed to delegate *part* of their jobs. . . . The purpose of delegation is to enable a manager to concentrate on his or her own job, not to delegate it away."

In the case of Jack's boss, she feels that she must do everything herself. Therefore, she can't help her employees develop their own talents and skills. A trained expert in hazardous waste management but with fewer years on the job than his boss, Jack could save his division chief time and energy by taking over some of the tasks that keep her running in circles and constantly checking on him. By not utilizing delegation, Jack's manager is limiting her own effectiveness, wasting the training and expertise of those whom she "tags after" in the department, and—worst of all—she is not giving her subordinates room to grow.

Delegation Isn't a Mechanical Process

Until the landmark study *The Effective Executive*, written by Dr. Drucker in the late sixties, delegation had been viewed as merely a mechanical process of routing the flow of work from managers to subordinates. But after Dr. Drucker's identification of the distinctive skills of the executive, ongoing psychological studies of corporations and their leaders have revealed that delegating as a management task involves more than a judiciously planned organizational chart. All types of factors impact on positive delegation, ranging from the economical and logical to the social and psychological. Although research is slim on the differences between men and woman managers in their use of the delegation process, many people claim that women supervisors have more of a problem in this area than men.

Says Katharine Graham, chairman of the board of The Washington Post Company, "Some women have a tougher time learning to delegate responsibility. In fact, learning to delegate is universally cited as one of the hardest adjustments to make moving up the corporate ladder. That, of course, is a problem for both sexes as they learn to manage. But the difference is . . . women were brought up to be conscientious, good girls and to take orders—not to give them."[2]

Many reentry women in the work force often carry their mothering tendencies with them into their new professional life. "A total disaster," says one male executive who requested anonymity in return for his frankness. "The homemaker with children who reenters the business world as a middle manager often practices mothering instead of delegating. She literally smothers her subordinates by doing their thinking for them, threatening rather than teaching, bribing rather than encouraging, and passing on to them minor, unpleasant details of her own job.

"She never really delegates. . . . Her management style is restrictive. She kills the initiative of any capable subordinate, for all her employees are encouraged to 'run to mother' for help with every minor problem. If they goof on any assignment, she takes over the job she gave them—no matter how insignificant it might be."

Professor Nathaniel Stewart, author and director of a consulting firm in organizational management, says, "When the climate is such that employees are fearful of making an error, it is unlikely that they will accept delegated tasks, no matter what authority the boss has. All a subordinate has to do is to bungle a delegated task once and he will not be called upon in the future."[3]

How to Convince Your Boss to Delegate

If you now work for a nondelegating woman manager, you have an uncommon challenge in front of you. In order to make your own job more stimulating and fulfilling, you have to convince your boss that delegation is a vital management tool, much broader than just accomplishing work through other people. Although her focus must still be on results—getting a job done on time and with budget and quality specifications—your manager must place an emphasis on enhancing your motivation. Or to put it another way, she must master the art of delegation in all of its nuances.

Dr. Trezzie A. Pressley, dean of the College of Business and Technology of East Texas State University at Commerce, Texas, says, "Positive delegation does not simply happen by itself. It is a management technique that requires a thorough understanding of the principles involved, a commitment to its use as a motivational tool, and a willingness to perfect its application through thoughtful practice. It is a result-and-motivation-oriented approach to making work assignments that succeeds only when managers understand and apply the key factors essential to its success."[4]

Help Your Manager Take the Big Step

If you are in a position like Jack, where your woman boss doesn't select you for a particular task that you are clearly qualified to perform, there are a few elementary steps that you might take that will help your supervisor decide what to delegate.

1. Make a personal list of all of the jobs that you know come under her aegis. Then sort out the activities you perceive as having a high potential for delegation to you. Depending upon your experience and training, these could range from simple chores like revising schedules and updating charts to more complex tasks such as drafting speeches or producing in-depth technical reports.
2. Secondly, identify each specific function that your boss performs on a frequent or regular basis. This might be a monthly report to her supervisor, a journal of future activities, an inventory of supplies, or two dozen other items that she could delegate without too much fear of losing control.
3. Lastly, now that you have itemized all of the varied activities currently handled by your manager, and also identified the routine functions that take up so much of her time, you are ready to determine which of these jobs could be delegated to you. With what assignment could you develop new skills, expand your knowledge, and apply your creativity in a challenging arena?

Professor Robert Maidment, of the College of William and Mary, offers this warning to bosses who fail to delegate and thus don't permit subordinates to develop their talents:

> If a manager doesn't teach his or her employees new skills, doesn't have high expectations for their performance, doesn't allow them to make mistakes while they are learning, doesn't responsibly monitor their efforts, and doesn't acknowledge their successes, then, that manager shouldn't expect them to consistently perform any job well.[5]

From this admonition to supervisors, you can readily understand why your last step is the most crucial. You now have to convince your woman manager to reserve for herself the tasks that only she can perform well and delegate the rest to subordinates like you.

Prepare to Be a Delegatee

This doesn't sound easy—and it isn't. Professor Earl Brooks says that in his management seminars at Cornell University, he has observed that women managers are less likely to seek and accept help from others, are less trustful, harder to convince, and are less likely to delegate.[6] Simply put, to persuade your female manager to delegate some tasks to you, you have to sell yourself. Your responsibility as a subordinate is to reassure your boss that you are prepared to be what Dr. Lawrence Steinmetz calls "the delegatee."

> Work cannot be effectively delegated unless the delegatee is prepared to handle it. This means that the delegatee must have acquired the training and experience needed to enable him or her to perform the task for which he or she will be held accountable. However, a note of caution on this point: Many people will use the excuse that they are not ready to undertake a specific task because they have not had sufficient experience. But it must be

> recognized that experience must be obtained for the first time in any person's life. . . .
>
> Certainly, a person who has not had sufficient training for it cannot be expected to perform a particular job. However, if a person has had sufficient training, but not "sufficient experience," there is no reason to withhold the assignment from him or her. In fact, if the subordinate is properly trained to do the job, this is the time to give him or her the opportunity to get the experience.[7]

In a recent study conducted by Professor Brooks, it was found that the most common excuse that managers give for not delegating is that the subordinates have less experience than the boss. "On the other hand," adds Dr. Brooks, "most managers readily agree that the best way to overcome this barrier is to provide opportunities for responsible work assignments with proper training and guidance. Although the subordinate might not handle an assignment in exactly the same way his superior would, he might do it even better. Remember, swimming can't be learned without getting into the water."[8]

Should your own experience be lacking, take heart, and help your manager delegate tasks to you. Management experts have found that employees who are allowed by their bosses to make their own decisions on how work will be performed show a marked improvement in motivation. By the very act of your boss delegating authority to you, you will be impelled to take a greater interest and pride in your work. Moreover, the same research indicates that delegation provides on-the-job training in making decisions, evaluating risks, and handling conflict.[9]

Lack of Experience Shouldn't Stop You

Assuming that you feel confident of your training even if you haven't had a great deal of experience, you will find the following strategies helpful in persuading your woman boss that you are indeed a candidate for delegatee:

1. Present yourself to her in a calm, confident manner. Use effective body language, and if you are a woman, keep your voice low-pitched and pleasant.

2. Carefully structure the way in which you ask for additional tasks. Remember, your manager feels solely responsible for everything and wants to keep all authority. Her reluctance to delegate could stem from any number of the following reasons—and, you should be cognizant of them:

- Lack of confidence in her ability to delegate.
- A fear that you might show her up with your competence.
- An insistence on perfection—maintaining that she is the only one who can perform the job right.
- An inner desire to be the martyr. Just picture a manager who beats her bosom as she swallows her third tranquilizer of the day and wails, "No one knows how overworked I am."
- Her fear of criticism by you or any of her subordinates. This type of boss dreads being blamed for a poorly conceived plan or for a foolish move. She would rather do the task herself than risk being the object of derision by her subordinates.

3. If you are aware of a minor problem that your boss hasn't found time to solve, offer to give her a written synopsis for a plan of action. When she evaluates your interpretation of the issue, casually tell her that you have a detailed blueprint for resolving the situation. If you have made it this far and she asks for your solution, congratulations are in order. For you have just made the plunge and eased your manager into the delegation process. When she realizes that you have taken a nagging headache off her hands and freed her for more important management functions, she will be able to overcome her reluctance to delegate.

4. After your supervisor finally delegates a particular task to you, don't, for goodness' sake, ever transfer responsibility back to her. This is known as "reverse delegation"[10] and it will short-circuit all of your efforts to gain responsibility and authority. When your boss hands you an assignment and says, "Let me

know if I can help," wave a thank you to her and head the opposite way. As Dr. Drucker puts it,

> The most serious problem with delegation occurs when the subordinate delegates the job back upward again. He unloads responsibility back onto the boss, and the boss just loves it. It flatters her because it says she is wise, able, indispensable. Very few bosses have the sense to recognize what's happening and say, 'Joe, that's your job. Do it yourself. Just keep me up on what you're doing.'[11]

A Boss Who Won't Let Go

Andy, a software engineer working for a contractor in defense satellite computer systems in Sunnyvale, California, is a key member of a three-man team that reports to Suzanne, a Harvard M.B.A. and "one hell of a woman," in his enthusiastic opinion. In response to my question, "What is she like as a boss—how effective are her skills?" I receive a barrage of answers, most focusing on the cut of her leather jeans. Finally, Andy strokes his luxuriant beard and says, "If only her ability to delegate was as terrific as her legs."

With a bit of encouragement, he fills me in on what he says Suzanne's male subordinates call their "pain in the ass problem" in private. "Our gorgeous boss likes to 'roam the range,' making client contact and doing the marketing for our division. That's great for the company, for she grabs attention wherever she goes. She's excellent with customers, always stressing the price and service we offer.

"The thing is, Suzanne doesn't know how to let go to achieve maximum efficiency from the superprofessionals who report to her. If she delegated specific work assignments to each one, instead of handing two of us the same identical project for fear that it might not get done, she'd be showing some real horse sense. Also, this would prove her faith in our capability of achieving the desired results. For God's sake, we're experts in our field!

"But we can live with the duplicate assignments. The critical issue among us guys is that we're delegated responsibility all the time, but without any true authority. Y'know, I might not have gotten my master's degree from Harvard, but I'll tell you, if I learned one thing in management seminars, it's never, never give your employee responsibility for performance without giving him or her the authority to direct the performance."

Suzanne is one step ahead of many women managers, for she does delegate and distribute the various jobs among her engineering team. This action in itself indicates that she has made an emotional/mental adjustment that is often difficult—or even impossible—for female bosses who have had sex-linked early jobs. Author Linda Downs says, "The 'I do it better syndrome' usually is the result of women starting out in detail-oriented work, of having found praise or challenge only in doing small tasks very well and, often, of feeling that they had to do everything perfectly, in order to prove that they were as good as male co-workers."[12]

Ask for Authority

If you, as a subordinate, are delegated responsibility for a project, you must make certain that you also receive the authority from your boss. Without this assurance of power, you merely end up as a yes-man or yes-woman. Although Andy and his team of software engineers are on top of their jobs, the men feel that they can neither develop nor progress because they aren't given even limited authority to take certain actions for the company on their own. "It's damned frustrating," explains Andy, "for with our boss's okay, we have shown our ability time and again to make the right decision. Hell, we know better than anyone else what we can and cannot offer to one of our customers."

An effective woman executive decides the extent of the authority she is willing to relinquish to her employees and then outlines the tasks for which each one is accountable. In case you are asking yourself, "How do I know how much authority to assume?" the answer is, "Ask your supervisor." Each manager has a different style of delegation, from the one extreme of the executive who turns over an assignment carte blanche to a subordinate, to the other extreme who treats her skilled subordinate as "an assistant to . . ." with virtually no responsibility or authority.

Authority Allows a Choice of Behaviors

Dr. James C. Harrison, Jr., offers an interesting view: "The degree of authority is dependent on the extent to which a person is allowed to substitute one behavior for another."[13] For instance, in this recent conversation that Andy had with his manager, Suzanne, it is obvious why the software engineer feels that he has responsibility without any real authority for the work that is delegated to him:

Suzanne: I'm going to hit L.A. for a marketing trip, Andy. I'll be gone until the end of the week. So I would appreciate it if you would take over the B.E. account while I'm away.

Andy: No problem, Suzanne. I'm familiar with all of their needs. I'll see that they receive the new programs that we've designed for their application and tell them if they run into trouble, they should buzz me. Could be that we'll have to ship some extra components for that system. Another possibility I foresee is that we'll have to free an engineer to fly there to fill them in on the new documentation. But don't worry, I'll stay on top of it.

Suzanne: Hold it, Andy! I would rather make the decision myself on additional parts as well as on the necessity for one of our engineers to help them out. I'll call you three times each day, and you can contact me in the evening if you have any problems. I'm getting a schedule together so you'll know when I'm due in from the meetings. If you can't reach me, leave a message at the hotel desk. This is a key account, and I want to be sure we don't lose it.

As you can see, Andy's boss delegated specific work to him with the responsibility to see that the project was carried through. But then she very effectively took back any authority that he had, before she left on her business trip. To understand the ramifications of her actions, note this definition of *authority* by Dr. Earl Brooks:

> Authority is the permission granted to take actions for or by the organization, usually within certain limits. Authority also is the right to use and commit resources of the organization and to make decisions required to meet responsibilities which the subordinate and his manager have agreed upon.[14]

One nationally recognized executive who says she perceived the value of delegation at the beginning of her career two decades ago is Claire Gargalli, president of Equibank, the highest ranking woman banking official in the country. She maintains, "I am a firm believer in effective delegation, for I am best when I can assemble the most creative, talented, and capable team who can work with me in accomplishing the job. Although I might give my team members full responsibility and complete authority, an executive can never delegate accountability."[15]

Ms. Gargalli's viewpoint is shared by virtually all knowledgeable business executives, no matter what style of delegation they use. As Dr. Harrison says, "Though an assistant can be vested with full responsibility and complete authority, the executive, nevertheless, cannot escape final, full accountability for the results."[16]

Help Your Manager Gain Confidence

Now that you have an appreciation of delegation as one of the primary keys to leadership effectiveness, you should evaluate how much positive delegation your boss practices. If it's minimal, you have already received earlier in this chapter a few techniques for luring her into delegating.

However, if you have a manager who is assigning you responsibility for certain tasks but is not giving you the authority to see them through, you know that your manager is at least aware of the need for delegation in the management function. She apparently has some sort of "delegation block" that makes her fearful of giving authority to a subordinate who has already been entrusted with the responsibility. You might try these strategies to turn her into an effective delegator:

1. When you receive an assignment from your supervisor, ask her to clearly define its scope. Check on goals for the project, deadlines, performance standards, time limits, materials available, manpower resources and budget availability. These parameters should then be written down, with duplicate copies available to both you and your boss. Make sure—by asking—that your boss has delegated to you the authority, the position, and the power (or influence) to do the job.
2. If you know that your manager has a fear of losing control if she delegates, assure her that you will maintain a control system so that she is kept informed of your progress at all times. Ask her how she wants this report given to her and when. When you are certain that your manager has both a need for achievement and a need to control, gently convince her that delegation leads to increased productivity.
3. Assure her that you will attempt to avoid any serious mistakes that might jeopardize the outcome of your task. Even though you and I know that surgeons and airline pilots are the only persons who never make errors —with the exception of the two of us—your boss doesn't believe this. She is convinced that every subordinate on her staff is capable of the ultimate mistake that will reflect back on her.
4. Offer to try on a few of her hats. Who knows? One might fit! Many bosses have a "multihat" syndrome, because their man-

agement functions are not clearly defined. When this happens, the manager tries to perform a dozen jobs alone and fails to concentrate on such management priorities as delegation.

5. If you find that she gives you work that is appropriate to your level of expertise but continues to check on you at all stages of the project, confront her with your feelings about this type of supervision. "Trust is the reciprocal of control," says Professor Robert Maidment, "Tight control frequently demonstrates weak trust; light control frequently demonstrates peak trust."[17] If your boss has delegated a task to you, she should let you complete it without wasting her time on repetitive checking.

When Equal Opportunity Hinders Delegation

Lois is a surprise! I always imagined Capitol Hill lobbyists to be cigar-chomping little men with pot bellies as round as grapefruits adorning their tight waistbands. Lois is chief lobbyist on the Hill for one of the nation's largest pharmaceutical houses, and the only adornment at her waist is a wide gold belt that sets off to perfection her simple black dress. She appears to be in her early forties. Crinkly laugh lines are around her eyes and gray-tipped ringlets frame her face.

"I hear that you had a strange experience as an executive before you came to Washington"—I immediately get to the point of my visit—"and, of course, as I promised on the telephone, I'll keep your identity and that of your company a secret if you tell me what happened."

Lois offers me a stick of sugarless gum from the pack she's unwrapping and replies, "I gave up smoking, and this is my substitute—like maybe ten packs a day. I've become a real gumaholic. Yes, to answer your question, I did have a most unusual three years as the first woman executive in a formerly male-run company. My corporation's response to the EEO ruling was to give me a title of vice president—I previously had been director of a tiny research department—but with little responsibility. The man who had earned the right to be given the title—legitimately—became one of the seven people who reported to me.

"The catch was, in the perception of top management he had the real authority. In separate meetings with our chief operating officer, we were asked to role-play for several years while they groomed me to be their lobbyist in D.C. This meant that the male with the experience stayed in the shadows while I was visible as the token woman manager. However, he called the shots and essentially ran the department."

Lois tells me that this weird charade went on for almost two years before she rebelled and took control. "I was afraid to delegate anything, for I didn't really feel in charge," she continues. "So I delegated 'nothing' jobs, never asking for feedback and not getting any. Then one day it all came to a head, when I met with one of our union presidents and he asked for a huge concession during grievance negotiations. I was floored and told him I would have to check with several of my bosses before we could sit down together and hammer out a contract. He became furious, wagged a nicotine-stained finger under my nose, and said, 'Young lady, you're negotating this contract with me. If you don't have the authority to say yes, for heaven's sake, go and get it. If you can't get it, don't waste my time anymore and find me somebody who is a real boss, dammit!'

"That tough old gent opened my eyes" Lois went on, "and at that moment I made up my mind that I was going to use the authority that came with my title—'legit' or otherwise. I knew that I couldn't function as a manager wearing ten different hats; therefore, one of my first objectives was to learn how to delegate to the seven people who reported directly to me. Obviously, when I took charge, the 'let's pretend' game ended. I think that I can say now, with all due modesty, that I am an expert on the art of delegation."

Lois shared with me some of the wisdom she gained about the proper way to delegate if you're a new woman manager.

Delegation Strategies for the New Woman Manager

1. Provide your subordinates with the opportunities and tools for developing themselves. This means giving them responsibility and authority for carrying out assigned tasks.

2. Don't oversupervise or overcontrol those who work for you. Your goal is to make them self-directed.

3. The larger your company in terms of numbers of employees, managers, and levels of supervisors, the more your need to delegate. You can't run a one-woman show if you have a hundred people under you. Adjust your management style as your firm grows, for it is impossible to retain an intimate knowledge of hundreds of employees in dozens of departments.

4. If passion should strike and you unexpectedly find yourself in a nine-to-five tizzy over your new male subordinate, choose an out-of-town assignment and quickly delegate it to him. This type of delegation might not reflect adequately your management expertise, but it should prevent what *The Harvard Business Review* calls "organizational chaos" erupting from a new type of office love affair.[18] Romance in the American corporation is serious business, says management guru Peter F. Drucker. "Nothing is more embarrassing in the workplace than a flirtatious woman boss. Both men and women become acutely uncomfortable."[19]

5. Treat your male and female subordinates as equally as possible when you delegate tasks. According to Dr. Drucker, "women managers tend to be very tough on women who report to them. They seem to adopt this stance, for they're out to prove that they aren't showing favoritism to one of their own sex."[20]

6. Establish minimal but effective controls for keeping track of the progress of your subordinates' work.

7. Never delegate projects that are unique to your skills and experience.

8. Delegate credit, but never publicly delegate blame to one of your subordinates. A good manager delegates wisely so that those who work for her are given credit for their accomplishments. When a project backfires, the final accountability rests with you, the manager.

Boss Assessment Questionnaire: The Manager Who Is an Ineffective Delegator

Evaluate your boss for her ability to delegate effectively with the following rating scale:

A—Always or yes	5 points for each A answer
S—Sometimes or occasionally	3 points for each S answer
R—Rarely or never	1 point for each R answer

1. Does your boss appear to be afraid that you will make mistakes if she delegates a task to you, even though you have the expertise in that particular area? ______

2. Do you believe that your manager is worried that you might do a job too well and show her up as not being as capable as you are? ______

   Then the question might arise: Why is she in charge if someone else is able to do the job better?

3. Does your boss seem to delegate only the "dog" work and keep the most interesting jobs for herself? ______

4. Does your boss show symptoms of overcontrol that block her ability to delegate effectively? ______

   These would include: numerous visits to each subordinate's office to check on the progress of certain jobs; frequent telephone calls; daily or even twice-daily staff meetings; dozens of interoffice memos with careful instructions for every phase of a job assignment; repeated checks on your financial outlay for a task that has been carefully budgeted; and an insistence on reviewing each completed task to make certain that it is perfect.

5. Do you feel that your woman supervisor is a little unclear about what her role is in the company? ______

   Management consultant and author Lin Bothwell sees this as a major barrier to delegation by a boss: "These individuals often feel that they have been given a job to do, a job that they are being paid for. They feel that having someone else do even part of their job would be inappropriate, unethical or even immoral."[21]

6. Does your female boss fail to communicate a management policy to you so that you never have enough information to make an informed decision and therefore are compelled to check with her on all issues? ______

7. Is your manager a "mad juggler," with five balls constantly in the air so that her days are filled with crises and panic situations—stamping out fires that could have been prevented by delegation? ______

8. Does your boss delegate tasks to her subordinates and then fail to give adequate instructions or clear parameters for establishing goals and achieving results?

   ______

9. Have you and your peers noticed that your manager appears to be permanently attached to a bulging briefcase that seems to accompany her home, to the ladies' room, to luncheon meetings, and possibly even to afterwork tête-à-têtes? ______

   This nondelegating boss is not only a martyr to her job, but she's wallowing in self-praise for taking on the workload of five subordinates!

10. After your boss delegates a task to you, does she then abandon you and fail to review your performance, ne-

glect to give you noncritical coaching, and overlook you for praise and financial reward? ______

11. Do you think that your boss is afraid to delegate for fear that she may lose some status as the manager who is capable of doing everything? ______

12. Does your supervisor constantly criticize everyone on her staff, claiming their collective incompetence prevents her from delegating anything of importance? ______

Total Score ______

60–45 Your boss has never learned to delegate properly.
45–29 Your manager has a fear of delegating tasks.
29–12 A toast to your boss! She can delegate wonderfully.

Chapter 7

The Nonlistening Boss

When Your Supervisor Tunes You Out

Marjorie was depressed and frustrated as she strolled out of the weekly staff meeting called by her boss, the features editor of an Atlanta daily. As her colleagues jostled past, anxious to return to the terminals at their desks in the huge city room of the paper, she headed for the coffee machine, mentally berating herself for not jumping in when her editor concluded the meeting with her usual cheery and meaningless challenge: "Any questions, gang? If not, see y'all at your word processors."

The young writer for the style section had a number of questions to ask her woman boss, but as always, her superior talked constantly for the entire hour without leaving even a minute to listen to the problems of her subordinates.

Taking the scalding cup of coffee with her, Marjorie sat down beside Janet, one of the food writers, and had the following conversation:

Marjorie: Every time I come away from one of these meetings, I feel as though the ground has been cut from under me. No matter what questions I want to bring up, she always monopolizes the whole darned session, and we're left hanging. Does it bother you that there is a total breakdown in communication between the six of us and our editor?

Janet: It sure as hell does. I've tried on a number of occasions to get a question in when she takes a breath or when she says "D'ya know?"—but it's useless. She's too concerned about meeting the afternoon deadline and trying to accomplish ten things at once. You can't talk on the phone, okay the day's assignments, and at the same time listen to your employees who have a problem. It's impossible. You're too damned preoccupied. So with all the distractions, you quit listening. And Marjorie, my friend, that's exactly what our dear boss is doing—just plain turning us all off! Or, as my grandpap used to say, turning a deaf ear when you don't want to listen.

Listening as a Management Tool

Listening, a complex, learned human activity that we all take for granted, has been, until the past decade, one of the least-understood and least-researched management tools in the workplace. Why? Because most managers, concerned about getting their messages across to those with whom they work, view the act of interpersonal communication as consisting of speaking, writing, or reading. Few supervisors see listening as part of the communication process, and fewer still recognize listening as a rare skill that must be mastered in the business world. According to author and researcher William Ford Keefe, numerous studies have concluded that most supervisors spend between 45 and 63 percent of their working day in the act of listening![1] For management trainees and students, listening time can consume 75 percent of their waking hours. Compare this with the fact that we spend 30 percent of our waking time speaking, 16 percent reading, and 9 percent writing.[2]

Although little research on listening was done prior to the fifties, the act itself traditionally has been considered a feminine attribute, of little or no value to the corporate sector. "Now," says Dr. Lyman K. Steil, founder and first president of the International Listening Association, "there is increased interest in listening as a vital key to career success. It is no longer possible to ignore the positive effect of good listening skills upon successful interactions in the workplace. Listening affects relationships between managers and their subordinates as well as between executives and their peers."[3]

Poor Listening Affects Work Relationships

Lance is an apprentice pastry chef in a classic French restaurant in the Old Town area of St. Augustine. A twenty-two-year-old graduate of an outstanding culinary institute, his goal is to manage his own gourmet dining spot. But first he must pay his dues by serving in various types of chef-assistant positions in restaurants and hotel dining rooms from coast to coast.

He's ecstatic in his new job, for his woman boss has given him permission to try his hand at exotic desserts—his favorite culinary exercise. But there is a caveat: he can't spend the amount of time that he feels he needs to lovingly prepare an individual *patisserie* for each customer. "Who wants to make them all look alike? Crass commercialism," he grumbles as he storms from the kitchen. He knocks on the closed door where Michelle, the executive chef, is working on the confectionery order for the following week.

Lance: May I please see you f—?

Michelle: Sure, come on in. You know, I've been meaning to ask you about those eggs that were delivered yesterday. Seems to me that they were a little aged, should we say? As though the hens that laid them were great-great-grandmothers.

Lance: Yeah, Michelle, you're probably right, but—

Michelle: You might think I'm too particular, but the ingredients are so important—you can't underestimate the necessity for obtaining the best.

Lance: Sure, but, I—

Michelle: Oh, I understand. You felt that so long as the eggs looked okay, we could use them. But always trust your nose,

Lance! A famous old chef told me that ten years ago, and I've never forgotten to sniff first.

Lance: (shouting in frustration) That's wonderful, Michelle, but I didn't come in here to talk about eggs. For God's sake! Can't you ever listen to anybody?

Michelle: You didn't say you—well, what the hell *do* you want?

Lance: Just forget it.

In this scenario, enacted thousands of times a day between managers and subordinates in all kinds of jobs, we see just a few of the effects of poor listening—alienation of employees; communication breakdown between boss and subordinate; and a probable loss of time and money because the manager did not pay attention to the subordinate's desire to spend hours crafting each individual dessert. Through her lack of listening, the women manager conceivably might lose a potentially creative employee, and the young man could give up a challenging opportunity to learn his trade.

Millions of Dollars Lost

Dr. Steil, founder and president of Communications Development, Inc., sees the fallout from ineffective listening as affecting managers and subordinates at all levels. He says, "With more than 100 million workers in this country, a simple ten–dollar mistake by each of them, as a result of poor listening, would add up to a cost of a billion dollars per year. And most people make more than one listening mistake every day. Ideas can be distorted by as much as 80 percent as they're stretched, condensed, twisted and hurried along the sometimes tortuous organizational path. The cost of that distortion is more than dollars. Letters have to be retyped, appointments rescheduled, shipments rerouted. Productivity is affected and profits suffer."[4]

If you have problems with a nonlistening woman boss like the editor in Atlanta or the executive chef with the bad eggs in Florida, remember, you're not alone. Everyone craves a good listener. The irony of poor listening is that although we all want an audience—even if it's just one person—tests reveal that most individuals do not listen well. Immediately after listening to a ten-minute presentation, the average listener has heard, correctly understood, properly evaluated, and retained only half of what was said. Within forty-eight hours, that drops to a final 25 percent effectiveness level![5]

From these statistics, compiled by Communications Consultants, Inc., of Minneapolis, you can understand why you feel alienated when your nonlistening manager doesn't even assimilate 50 percent of what you are attempting to communicate. On a much more positive note, however, there is overwhelming evidence that, with systematic, focused, and directed effort, listening can be improved.[6]

Listening Skills for Your Boss

You might try these tactics for helping your woman supervisor gain better listening skills:

1. Clarify in your own mind what you want to convey to your boss before you meet with her. She will be more receptive if your ideas are crystallized and you are certain of what you intend to accomplish by your conversation. All experts agree that listening well is difficult, for people can speak only 100 to 200 words per minute, but your mind is capable of thinking two to six times that fast.[7] Thus, your boss is racing ahead of your conversation, letting her mind wander to a weekend trip and undoubtedly losing most of what you're saying.

2. Start with the assumption that listening is not a natural skill. It is a learned activity, and if your boss has a weakness in this area, it is going to take time and effort on your part to help her. As Dr. Steil says, "Our listening behaviors have been acquired

and reinforced over a long period of time, so that adult listening behaviors are habitual."[8]

3. When you plan to speak with your supervisor, don't just trudge into her office any old time. Set up a meeting and give her some idea of what you want to discuss. Psychologically, she'll then be ready to listen to you.

4. Before your meeting, scout out the area for obvious hindrances that might prevent her from listening to you. Noise obstructions can be the worst: pounding typewriters, ringing telephones, sputtering air conditioners, or loud carpentry can hamper the listening process. Just imagine expecting your boss to listen to you over the incessant noise of a jackhammer outside her window. If you're aware of such impediments to the listening process, suggest getting together in another office.

5. Avoid meeting with your boss in a space where there are physical obstacles to your making effective eye contact with each other. This could mean large executive desks, sofas, easy chairs, or the conference room table—almost any oversize object in the office that creates a barrier between you. As a subordinate, you are then made to feel that the boss is avoiding contact with you and keeping her own space inviolate. Take a tip—meet your manager for breakfast before the business day begins, or converse with her in an informal "neutral" place.

6. Try not to "overtalk" when you finally meet with your manager. Keep your conversation brief, concise, and to the point.

7. Be careful of any "semantic" barriers that you might unwittingly erect when you attempt to improve your supervisor's listening habits. Because of the very words you use in a conversation, your female boss might not understand your point, could be offended, or might even "tune you out." "A very common situation," say William G. Callerman and William McCartney. They explain: "Listening can be affected when different people give different meanings to the same word, depending on their background. For example, to a European, a 'Yankee' is an American; to a member of the Boston Red Sox, a 'Yankee' is a member of a rival baseball team, and to a Southerner, a 'Yankee' is a Northerner."[9]

Watch Your Timing!

The importance of choosing the proper moment to get the best listening performance from your woman boss is critical. Remember these strategies:

1. If you know that she's a coffeeholic, wait until she has had that first cup in the morning to speak to her. She will be more awake, in a relaxed state of mind, and better prepared to listen.
2. Don't approach her with your problem the moment she walks into the office. Let her have time to sort through the mail, answer urgent telephone calls, and get into the rhythm of the workplace.
3. Try to avoid asking for a meeting first thing Monday morning or during the last hours of Friday afternoon. Your manager's mind will not be on your problem at the beginning of the week because she has a dozen areas of work she must cover. And on Friday, she might be planning an evening out, a Sunday brunch, or a lazy time beside the pool. She could be distracted, and her listening abilities will be tuned to "off."
4. When your supervisor is preparing for an out-of-town conference or even a short vacation, you had better hold your conversation for when she returns. Our normal tendency to "clean everything up" before leaving for a period away from the office precludes effective listening. Your manager will be concentrating either on a speech she is to present or on the availability of hotel rooms at the shore. Don't assume that she will be understanding or responsive to what you have to say.
5. Stay away from launching a persuasive appeal to your supervisor when you know that she has just finished a rough go-around with her own boss. She could vent her frustration on you because her manager, the executive vice president, failed to listen to her!
6. If your boss is a creature of habit—as most of us are—and you are mindful that she leaves for lunch each day at twelve

noon, don't bring up an important question just before she heads out the door. Her growling response probably will come from an empty stomach rather than from a reasoned and thoughtful approach.

7. Avoid entering into a situation where your boss must listen closely to you when you know that she has personal problems or other distractions. She can't be an effective listener when her mind is centered on a sick child or an out-of-work husband.

Men and Women Listen Differently

Gender differences in the way men and women listen are attributed primarily to the different upbringing of the sexes. Research indicates that males hear facts, picking up general ideas and conclusions, while females are more aware of the mood of a communication. Women, relegated traditionally to supportive roles as "helpers," have been expected by society, says Carl Weaver, "to display a listening style that is passive, submissive and distracted easily by outside forces."[10]

Over the past two decades, as sex roles have undergone dramatic changes in our society, our perspective of the art of listening has changed as well. Now recognized as an indispensable skill in the business world, with entire texts devoted to its ramifications, effective listening has expanded beyond the traditional gender barriers and is considered an integral part of management training. There is no question that you, as a subordinate reporting to a woman supervisor, must understand *what* your boss hears and *why* she hears it.

Do female managers listen differently from male managers? Absolutely, claim many experts. The disparity starts in childhood and continues up the corporate ladder, explains Professor Melanie Booth-Butterfield of Central Missouri State University: "Listening patterns show males and females differ in a number of ways: their goals in listening, to whom they listen, and in their basic abilities in listening. As more women occupy positions at all levels in organizations, these differences become increasingly critical for those who report to them. For instance, as your woman boss responds to the nonverbal cues she picks up as you converse—your tone of voice, rate of speaking, volume, emphasis, and even your physical appearance—she might miss out on more factual information."[11]

Nonverbal Cues Can Be a Turn-Off

Ted was on top of the world. He had just landed his first job—teaching English in a prestigious New England school—after a disheartening months-long search. Excited over the prospects ahead, he smiled at his fifth graders and handed out homework assignments. Meanwhile, packing up his own briefcase, he decided to stop in the principal's office to tell her about his idea for a celebration in honor of the anniversary of the Boston Tea Party.

Books under his arm and brilliant yellow striped shirt open at the collar, Ted was ushered into his boss's office by her secretary. He immediately began to outline his plan for the celebration, but he noticed that the principal kept glancing at her watch, riffling papers on her desk, and staring through him with an unresponsive air. Obviously, he thought to himself, something is bothering her and she's not interested. Under the continuing chilly gaze of his supervisor, his enthusiasm began to wane and his voice slowed. He finally apologized lamely for what he called his "stupid suggestion" and hastily left her office. He was bewildered. Why wasn't she enthusiastic about his idea?

After Ted walked out, the principal called in her secretary.

Principal: That vision in gold is our new English teacher! Did you see his impossible attire? I should have said something to him, but I was too shocked. At this school we all dress appropriately.

Secretary: What did he want?

Principal: How would I know? Something about celebrating

the Boston Tea Party. Truthfully, all I could think about was his garish shirt, and what an impossible role model he is for our youngsters.

Secretary: Perhaps his suggestion had some merit. The boys and girls seem to like him.

Principal: When someone dresses like that, they usually aren't worth listening to.

Here is a case where a teacher's innovative idea was thrown out by his female boss because she didn't listen to the factual message. She instead picked out the nonverbal cue of a "loud" shirt to turn off her listening capabilities. Many people do this in order to rationalize their bad listening behavior, according to author Ralph Nichols. "When someone talks to them, they mentally criticize either physical appearance or speech delivery, or both. The defects become excuses for not listening. . . . The listener becomes too critical of clothing, cosmetics, shoeshines, hairdos and so on and assumes, 'Anyone who looks like that can't have much to say.' "[12]

Your woman boss is far more likely to act in this way than a male manager because of her pattern of socialization in our society. Professor Booth-Butterfield says this type of listening has "enormous implications in the workplace." She adds, "Women going into business, industry, and government may have learned to listen for the inappropriate messages or learned to listen in inefficient, non-assertive ways."[13]

On the other hand, males sort out much of what they hear and listen selectively—particularly to females. This "tune-out and ignore" tendency of men toward women worries Dr. Booth-Butterfield because of its impact on the new woman manager. "Female executives or group leaders may not be listened to as carefully as their male counterparts, which can hurt their effectiveness and, ultimately, lead to confusion and possible failure of their subordinates."[14] To put it bluntly, research indicates that men listen closely to other men, but only superficially to women.

Listening Skills Can Be Learned

The higher you advance in management, the more critical your listening abilities become. Dr. Steil told *U.S. News & World Report*, "The most common problems in business arise when management doesn't listen to something that their workers are trying to tell them."[15] However, just because you consider yourself a subordinate, don't shirk your responsibility to become a good listener. Particularly if you are a male starting your first job, you probably will have to train yourself consciously to listen effectively, should you have a woman manager. Remember, you have been brought up to listen more attentively to men all your life.

Professor Booth-Butterfield says, "Entry level females can experience even greater problems than males. If you have just entered the work force, you may need special assistance in learning how to listen for task-oriented messages from your boss, a skill that women have been socialized to ignore."[16] Whether you are male or female, it will help if you consciously practice these proven listening skills:

1. Focus your attention on what your boss is saying.
2. Repeat to yourself the message you're receiving.
3. Paraphrase the instructions you're getting.
4. Put the messages you are hearing into a meaningful context so you will have better retention of the facts.
5. Learn to ask in-depth questions to enhance your listening effectiveness.

If you want to become a really good listener, you must do more than merely *hear* what your manager is saying. Dr. Steil says that communication involves three additional components: (1) *Interpretation* of what's said, which leads to understanding or misunderstanding; (2) *Evaluation*, which involves weighing the information and deciding how to use it; and (3) *Responding*, based on what you heard, understood, and evaluated. Above all, you must become an active listener so that you can mentally strike a bargain with your boss—a bargain based on your belief that you will always disagree agreeably with her in order to keep the lines of communication open. If you listen to your supervisor and she listens to you, the job is going to get done and done correctly the first time around.[17]

How to Listen to Your Manager

But what if you, rather than your woman boss, have a listening problem? Inasmuch as communication is a two-way street, it is necessary that you assume an active role in improving your own listening, not only for the immediate relationship with your manager, but for your future success. Dr. John L. DiGaetani, a nationally recognized authority on business communications, says, "The effects of really good listening can be dramatic. These effects include the satisfied customer who will come back, the contented employee who will stay with the company, the manager who has the trust of his staff, and the salesman who tops his quota."[18] If you want to cultivate better listening habits, take a few of these steps in the next several months:

1. Become an active listener. This means focusing on what your boss is saying and adapting your listening to the organization of her message. Try not to be distracted by external events or by your wandering thoughts of a cheeseburger and fries.
2. Make mental notes of your manager's message and, if practical, write yourself a brief synopsis of what she said. When time is short, jot down key words to jog your memory. If you're like most of us, remind yourself to write clearly in English so that you can read your notes later. Scribbles that resemble ancient Sanskrit aren't of much use in a modern office.
3. Look alive! Ask a question of your manager that will lead to amplification of what she has said. Linda Jane Colman and Susan Rawson Zacur advise: "This question should be neutral,

non-judgmental and non-accusing; it should seek only to keep the conversation flowing along the theme already established."[19]

4. Recognize any assumptions you might be making about what your manager is telling you. Often, many of us will take a giant leap from the actual facts of a message to inferences that are merely our own personal conclusions based on what we heard. There is nothing inherently wrong with this kind of listening as long as you realize that your response comes from assumptions and not from facts. The best precaution is for you to ask questions about your perceptions so misunderstandings don't occur.

5. Be aware at all times of your own perceptual filtering. Any words spoken to you pass through your individual "filter"—a personal frame of reference based on your past life experience. Since no two persons have the same personal experiences, your own filters can cause you to respond to your manager's message with anger, sadness, concern, or disbelief. Whatever emotion you experience can then color your perceptions of what your boss is saying.

6. When you are listening to your boss, be cognizant of each individual's need for "personal space." Most men and women don't mind sitting in close proximity to each other during a lunch or lecture, but when you meet individually with your manager, allow for some "air space" between you. In Western cultures, a lack of personal space can be very disconcerting and can adversely affect communication with your woman boss. If you are a male reporting to a female manager, allow a larger circle around your chair. When you move in too closely, your boss could interpret this as an act of intimidation or as a subtle sexual overture. Of course, if romance is your goal, then forget the personal space and take the shortest route to intimacy.

A New Manager Learns Listening Skills

Joellen, marketing director and head of the box office for a summer repertory theater, tells me of her struggle to acquire effective listening skills as we sip a soft drink in a cool, shaded valley in the Poconos. The evening performance of Bernard Slade's perennial hit, *Same Time, Next Year,* has just opened, and the twenty-three-year-old theater student has some free time before intermission.

"We're a small company," she says, "but they believe in marketing. I have two writers reporting to me, a group sales director, and a high school junior as my assistant in the box office. Last year was horrible—all my fault—I just didn't listen to what people were telling me. For instance, one night we had fifty-five Rotarians booked for dinner and an evening performance. My group sales director reported this to me as I was counting the matinee receipts. Her message didn't register—kind of in one ear and out the other—and I took a reservation two hours later for two hundred women from the local Baptist senior citizens center. What a catastrophe. We can fit only two hundred in the theater, so we had angry Rotarians hanging from the rafters and sweet white-haired old ladies shaking their umbrellas at them."

As she recalled the fiasco caused by her poor listening, Joellen almost spilled her soda from laughing. "It sure wasn't funny at the time, but you should have seen those men and women glaring at each other before the performance."

She admits that it was a minor miracle that the administration didn't fire her. "I was the world's worst listener. I had major disasters for the entire first month that I worked here—all because I was depending on the people who reported to me to be responsible for my getting the message. Fortunately, the owner of the summer theater called me in one morning and read me the riot act. He said, 'Learn to listen, or you're finished.' That did it. I loved the job and the people. So I devised all sorts of ways to listen. And it worked."

Strategies for Your Listening Success

Joellen's strategies are simple. If you are in a new management position, you might experiment with the following tactics, which saved her job:

1. Analyze your own strengths and limitations in listening.
2. Eliminate those behavior patterns that contribute to your poor listening habits.
3. When you are busy and a subordinate has something to tell you, stop what you're doing and listen. If this isn't possible, set up an appointment when you can discuss the issue without any distractions.
4. Concentrate when someone speaks to you.
5. If your thoughts run ahead of what your subordinate is saying, don't daydream! Take advantage of the extra minute and review what you have been told, evaluate the message, and anticipate what is coming next.
6. Obtain the entire picture quickly; eliminate the unessential facts.
7. Either paraphrase what you have been told or repeat the facts to someone else in the next few hours. Repetition will reinforce your memory of the conversation.
8. Remember that males and females listen differently. Compensate for your own gender-related listening habits.
9. Until you learn to listen well, take notes carefully and follow through on each conversation.
10. Don't depend on the other person for the success of the dialogue. Take responsibility for your own listening capabilities.
11. Keep your emotions in check. Anger, disgust, irritation, or any violent emotion will turn off your listening skills.

Boss Assessment Questionnaire: The Manager Who Lacks Listening Skills

Evaluate your supervisor for a nonlistening style using the following rating scale:

A—Always or yes	5 points for each A answer
S—Sometimes or occasionally	3 points or each S answer
R—Rarely or never	1 point for each R answer

1. Is your boss inclined to do a lot of talking and very little listening to you or your peers? ______
2. Do you feel that your manager fails to focus on what you are saying because she is trying to do too many things at once—signing letters, answering phone calls, doodling on a notepad? ______
3. When you are giving your boss a message or explaining your views, do her eyes appear to wander as she repeatedly attempts to interrupt you with questions that haven't any relevance to what you are telling her? ______
4. Does she consciously take over the conversation and try to thwart you from adding your viewpoint? ______
5. If you have a relatively relaxed conversation, does your woman manager turn the most innocuous interaction into a contest where you both become adversaries? ______
6. Does your boss appear to listen only when a topic has value for her or is easy to understand without too much effort? ______
7. Do you feel that your supervisor has a closed mind to ideas or suggestions put forth by her subordinates? ______
8. Does your boss go off on mental tangents and *fake* attention as you try to speak to her? ______

9. Does your female boss think she knows what you're trying to say even before you've finished talking, so that in her hurry she misses part of your actual message? _____

10. Does your manager fail to give you the courtesy, respect, and thoughtfulness that you should expect in a normal business environment? _____

11. Do you feel that your supervisor is often unprepared to discuss a particular topic and thus ignores any comment you might make about the issue? _____

12. Does your boss fail to accept what should be her 51 percent responsibility for communication success, regardless of her being the listener? _____

Total Score _____

60–45 Ship your boss off to a training program in effective listening.
44–29 Your manager is listening only with one ear.
28–12 Your boss listens to her subordinates reasonably well.

Chapter 8

The Decision-Maker

Who Wants to Take a Risk?

"Don't just stand there, dammit! Can't you get your boss to move? We're on deadline, and as usual, she's busy foot-dragging." The head of the print shop impatiently hovered over Maria's shoulder, watching her sketch a layout for a college catalog while, at the same time, trying to get her to approach her indecisive woman manager for overdue artwork. Muttering to himself, "Typical female, can't make up her mind," the printer lit a cigar, picked up several pieces of pastel from the floor, and stared belligerently across the room at the art director.

Oblivious to everyone's impatience, Maria's manager was shoving photos around, worrying about the aesthetics of a page. "How about this? Noooo, don't like that—perhaps another pic might look better. Or maybe if I slanted it that way . . . ? Boy, could I use an extra hour to play with this! But what the hell, gotta make a choice sometime—so let's go with the page the way it is."

The printer breathed an audible sigh of relief as the art director walked toward him. He grabbed the completed layout and ran from the office, obviously agitated by the boss's widely acknowledged problem with decision making.

Decision making is inherently one of the riskiest tasks that your manager has. You have discovered, I am sure, in the choices you make daily, that decisions often have a nasty habit of falling through, turning out bad, or ricocheting back at you in an unexpected manner. Professor Peter F. Drucker says, "Effective managers do not make a great many decisions." He adds, "They want impact rather than technique; they want to be sound rather than clever . . . and unless a decision has degenerated into work, it is not a decision. It is at best a good intention."[1]

For years, the stereotype of the woman as a non–decision maker has been rampant in our society with humor and innuendos similar to those of the printer directed at "the female who can't make up her mind." Research over the years has shown that "there are psychological differences in the way in which males and females carry on decision making, but on the whole, there is little significant difference in their innate abilities to make decisions."[2]

Decisions Put You in Charge

As might be expected, male/female upbringing in our society is once again cited as the villain. Male executives, characterized as strategists, team players, and planners, generally are perceived as confident risk takers and decision makers. Women managers, defined by their "little girl" gender roles as passive creatures who "view risk as entirely negative,"[3] often carry this female cultural experience into decision making. For you, their subordinate, this can be disastrous. Decision making is one of the most important actions you should expect from your boss. Luther Wade Humphreys and William A. Shrode say, "Decision-making is such an important activity that organizational success is largely dependent upon the ability of managers to consistently make sound decisions."[4]

Author Theodore Isaac Rubin goes even further than Dr. Humphreys in maintaining that the decisions we make—or fail to make—often determine the direction of our lives. "Decisions put us in charge of our own lives," he says. "Every time we make a real decision, we find out who we really are, because we make use of our own priorities and values. On the other hand, difficulty with decisions complicates all aspects of our lives. . . . There are many people who have great difficulty making decisions; some cannot make decisions at all. But however impeded or healthy, no free adult can avoid decision making."[5]

Is This Typical of Women Managers?

Martha, a psychiatric social worker at a mental health facility in Scottsdale, Arizona, is often confused by her manager's inability to decide various issues that affect their entire department. "My boss just hasn't a smidgen of confidence in her ability to solve everyday problems. Honestly, they're not even earth-shaking. Just last week she checked with each one of us on whether we wanted to work late because her program was backed up. The whole issue is absurd, a minor thing that she could solve herself without drawing all of us into it." Martha then described the conversation with her manager:

Boss: As you know, Martha, at this time of the year, when outpatients increase, our workload gets out of hand. What is your feeling about working overtime three nights a week?

Martha: Well, it's up to you. Naturally, my boyfriend would prefer that I kept the evenings for him, but if you really need me, I'll stay.

Boss: To be honest, I haven't made up my mind. I could ask for temporary help from the administrator of our division, but I hate to train new people and then have to let them go in a month.

Martha: I truly don't mind working an extra two hours several times a week, but I would like to know ahead of time, so I can make plans.

Boss: Oh, no problem with that, Martha. I should be able to make a decision in the next ten days—after I hear everyone's

> preference and try to figure if we can catch up some other way. Maybe I really don't have to hire anyone and we can streamline our operation a bit. I'm just not sure what I'm going to do.

Following this frustrating conversation with her uncertain boss, Martha felt angry and let down. Wouldn't you, if your manager were so indecisive? When you are subjected to this type of treatment from a female superior, it makes you insecure and unable to evaluate your alternatives or plan ahead. In addition, the procrastination tends to confuse you—you're really not certain just how much authority your boss has or whether it's your responsibility to offer positive input to her decision-making process.

Behavioral therapist Sylvia Senter explains, "Part of being a good executive is being decisive, because people are looking to you for guidance and policymaking. But many women have difficulty making decisions because other persons—parents, husbands—have been making decisions for them. They haven't had the opportunity to develop decision-making skills. Sometimes the things that may be keeping you back from making decisions are fear of making mistakes or taking risks, always wanting to be right, fear of disapproval, or wanting everyone to like you."[6]

Why Your Boss Can't Make Decisions

In order for you to learn how to become an effective decision maker yourself, it is important that you analyze why your woman boss has problems. If you believe that her inadequacies are not attributable to gender, look elsewhere for factors contributing to her poor decision making. At times, nebulous management guidelines or improper delegation by *her* boss play a role, and she has to deal with:

1. Vague lines of authority so that she is uncertain what power she has to implement decisions. If she can't get the necessary support from other levels of management, she won't feel any

urgency to make a decision and will probably let the matter drift.

2. Inadequate or confusing data given to her by her superiors. If what she is handed is inaccurate, she will become distrustful and fail to make any decisions at all. For instance, how can your boss make decisions on a particular job if she doesn't know labor costs, acceptable standards, and definite deadlines for completion of the various stages of a project?

3. A demoralizing workplace atmosphere that doesn't encourage independence and confident decision making. Your manager must have the privilege of being wrong sometimes, and so must you!

4. Uncertainty about the level of responsibility her boss has delegated to her for carrying a job through to conclusion. If she is befuddled about her responsibility, just imagine how she feels about her accountability! Particularly, if the decision-making power is split between two departments and several managers. It is a well-established fact that on the average, a significant area of confusion—ranging up to 25 percent—exists between the superior and subordinate as to what are the subordinate's true responsibility and accountability.[7]

Prove That You Can Be A Problem Solver First

Although decision making in the workplace is considered a managerial function, it must be practiced in varying degrees at all levels of any organization. Thus, it is important that you, the subordinate, learn to become a problem solver as proof that you are worthy of some degree of management responsibility. If you are a woman and haven't yet knocked down the "no trespassing" sign that keeps you from the managerial suite, take the first step and position yourself for line management. For it is in this area that you will be concerned with the factors that count—productivity, profits, and company growth. It is here, too, where you will face unanticipated problems, unforeseen financial losses, or overwhelming crises—all requiring decisions. As you learn to handle these with confidence, you will be able to dispel the still-persistent stereotype of the female who is afraid to be a decision maker.

Dr. Nathaniel Stewart, management consultant and author, sees women as "doubly deprived" in being restricted from line technical positions and management ranks. He explains,

> Since both offer a "ringside" view of the continuing scene of company problems, and of approaches used in dealing with these problems, women have been deprived of an important vantage point. Sex stereotyping of jobs has boxed them in at office desks or in other minor roles distant from the problem solving front, keeping them estranged from the environment where problems germinate and where problem solving and decision-making are most active.[8]

Sam, a thirty-year-old broker with the Albuquerque office of a national investment firm, isn't concerned about a line position, for he's all set to become a partner in his father's company after several years of "breaking in." But meanwhile, he reports to a woman manager whose instinct for choosing the right stocks at the right time has made her a legend among the "bulls." Her intuitive choices on the Big Board don't impress Sam, however. "I admire her instinctive 'feel' for the market, but she's driving us bananas with her decision-making style. We all have to depend upon her to do many things—signing forms or checks, taking our proposals to a higher level, okaying certain letters, or just signing memorandums to another division. She either stalls or stonewalls our efforts—often until it's too late. The strange part is, she usually appears to be in agreement with what we feel is needed, but then she puts off the decision—either it's 'too risky,' 'it might hurt someone,' 'no time to think it over'—and on and on. When it comes to budgetary decisions—she's hopeless."

If you report to a woman boss who has difficulty with decision making, there are many coping strategies you can use. But before you attempt any, understand that your manager may be worried, depressed, or guilty over her inability to make effective decisions. Your role, as the subordinate, is to help her understand the real reasons why she is avoiding decision making. For example, here is Sam speaking to his manager:

Sam: I'd like to handle the Grimes portfolio myself. I've been following it very closely, and I think I can do a good job.

Boss: Yes, I think you *could* possibly take it over. I'll have to give it some thought.

Sam: Do I hear that you have some doubt? I really want the responsibility. Perhaps you can give me the reasons why you think I'm not ready, and I'll work on them. Then in a few weeks, I should be ready to move.

Force a Decision from Your Woman Boss

If *you* aren't the problem, then identify the central issue that is causing your boss's indecision, and ask her in a sympathetic way to articulate it. Remain cool and attempt to look at her problem from a number of different angles—try to see it through her eyes. Meanwhile, obtain as much information as you can about what is troubling her, and consider every possible solution. According to Eugene J. Benge, international business consultant, "There is no single decision theory. Instead, there are various techniques, devices, and viewpoints for weighing possible courses of action. All are designed to increase fact gathering and decrease risk."[9]

After you have evaluated your options and you feel the time is right to risk approaching your boss, submit to her in writing the course of action that you feel is best for the issue. The following is a guideline for organizing your "decision-inducing" proposal:

1. Objective. Clearly define your manager's problem as you see it.
2. Proposal. Offer an outline of your solution and your perception of how it can be implemented.
3. Explanations. List all of the reasons why you feel that your new idea will work.
4. Plan. Detail, in consecutive order, how you feel your changes should be acted upon.
5. Expense Involved. This is difficult, but you should be able to come up with a ballpark figure for your solution that would

be applicable for a reasonable period of time. Remember, research indicates that "female managers experience the most difficulty with budgetary decisions."[10] Consequently, some women bosses do not relish challenging or unpleasant decision-making tasks related to money matters. For this reason, make certain that the costs you project are well-defined for the solution to your manager's problem.

6. Time Parameters. Estimate how long it will take for information gathering and for the completion of the project. Thus, by following this meticulous model, your manager can proceed with the decision-making process that you have literally outlined for her.

Don't be complacent if you have brought your indecisive boss to the point where you feel she is capable of decision making. "Plan some person-to-person follow-up contacts," says Dr. Robert Bramson. "It might even be needed the very next day," he adds. "By making these follow-up contacts with your boss, you are giving support . . . and dispelling resistance or internal conflict that may have developed overnight. If at all possible, keep the initiative for action in your own hands. . . . Otherwise, your manager will procrastinate indefinitely."[11] By taking your boss through these various stages, you should be able to help her translate her indecision into decisive action.

When a Woman Boss Impedes Your Progress

Both male and female subordinates claim that one of the most agonizing decisions in the workplace is whether to stick with a well-liked woman boss or to look elsewhere for a job because of her lack of clout within the organization. Says one male executive with a consumer products firm, who asked not to be identified, "It's not a myth—as some feminists claim—that women generally aren't going to be well integrated into line positions within an organization. It's reality. And unless this woman is a superstar, she's far less likely to move up and almost certain never to be the future president or chief executive officer of the corporation.

For this reason, men feel—and rightly so—that their opportunities for advancement under this woman manager are far less."

Obviously, this fear never surfaces with entrepreneurs like Barbara Proctor, who founded the Chicago advertising firm of Proctor and Gardner, or with executives who have inherited control of a family organization, such as Katharine Graham of The Washington Post Company. But it's a very real concern applicable to women managers who have worked their way up in a corporation or business.

Corroborating the perception that ambitious subordinates often have less chance for career growth with a female boss is James D. Johnson, vice president for Industry, Government Relations, and Lobbying for the General Motors Corporation. "Years ago," he says, "I had an excellent woman boss, but she had reached her limit at the middle-management level. So I had to make a very difficult decision to leave the company in order to move ahead in my own career."[12]

Presently, Mr. Johnson reports directly to Dr. Marina vN. Whitman, vice president, group executive in charge of public affairs staffs and chief economist for General Motors Corporation. "A top professional and outstanding person," he says of his manager, the first woman executive at GM. "The more people like her become involved and visible in corporate America, the sooner we'll see women making it to the top and heading large companies."

Dr. Whitman offers this advice to aspiring women executives: "If you're to be an effective manager, you're going to be a decision maker or go down the tube." She adds, "Subordinate men and women should have the same expectations for all managers—clarity of direction, fair evaluation and treatment, and honesty. Above all, I tend to deal candidly with people who work for me."[13]

Limited Choices

In some decisions, the alternatives are obvious from the beginning. For instance, if you're job hunting, you're going to apply only to the limited number of companies that hire people with your skills. In other decisions, you might have too many choices. In still other decisions, the choices not only are limited but are often loaded with serious drawbacks. And these are usually the type that face your woman manager who has difficulty with decision making. In order to help her when she feels that she's searching for answers from a limited number of choices, you might try these brainstorming strategies developed by major corporations:

1. Write down as many alternatives as you can for her problem. Consider all ideas initially, and don't, when you first draw up your list, throw out any that seem too unconventional.
2. Let your imagination soar, and try to be creative. Occasionally, unusual possibilities will turn out to be practical ideas when you discuss them with your woman manager.
3. If your boss seems to have an either-or decision for a particular situation, you should try to see if you can take a broader view of her problem. Your supervisor may be too close to an issue or too uptight about the impending decision to perceive alternative choices.
4. Consider the consequences of your suggesting alternatives to your manager, and be very certain that you list them in writing. Whatever it takes—a financial balance sheet or a report card system grading the choices—should be clearly shown along with the alternatives, to help her with decision making.

Throughout this chapter, you have learned abut the problems faced by your boss as an "individual" decision maker, but more and more, women managers say they are utilizing group decision making in their positions. Although familiar folk advice warns us, "Too many cooks spoil the broth," a number of women managers around the country prefer another adage: "Two heads are better than one." Jane Evans, president of Monet Jewelers, calls her management style "participatory," adding "I like a consensual approach to decision making. This gives me a win/win situation with our more than 1,800 employees. With this managerial style, women can bring a new dimension to the workplace."[14]

Echoing Ms. Evan's view of the woman executive's role in decision making is Christie Hefner, president and chief operating officer of Playboy Enterprises. "I think the most overwhelming truism is that everyone manages differently, but I personally use a less formal, less hierarchical form of management than most male chief executives. I prefer a cooperative, consensual way of managing. I would hope that these qualities find their way into the fabric of my corporation."[15]

Women Bosses and Their Lovers

Scott inhales the familiar, musky scent of Gail's cologne even before a featherlight touch on the nape of his neck tells him that his boss is standing behind his chair. "Scott, baby," she purrs in her husky voice, "you've worked long enough this evening. How about sharing a little nightcap while we go over plans for the on-site meeting with the state people tomorrow?"

A "true romance" out of a dime-store novel? Of course not! It's merely an inside view of the everyday office, where romance is as much a part of the contemporary working scene as government regulations, hostile takeovers, and foreign competition. The new twist that demands effective decision making is the liaison between you, a youthful subordinate, and your powerful, exciting woman boss—eight or ten years your senior. Are you turned on by your sexy manager? Naturally! After all, she's single, shares the same interests as you, and holds your future in her capable hands.

In years past, working women usually were in the playmate role, not considered the social equals of their male lovers. Easily discarded by the executive after a brief sexual fling, the female was considered an unlikely mate for the top male, and for the most part, the short-term relationship had little impact on the organizational structure. Today, when the determined, career-focused executive woman wants a partner, chances are good that he's going to be in the office, accompanying her on business trips, and helping her on a last-minute deadline. When you suddenly discover that your well-hidden interest in your boss is returned by her, that adrenaline high you shared with each other on an important project can be, according to authors Patrice and Jack Horn, "easily translated into sexual attraction."[16] After all, you're not only emotionally receptive, but your female executive has more freedom, power, and money than you. In addition, there is that constant professional interaction between you and the one person who can understand all the problems that confront you in the office.

The new workplace relationships can have a dramatic impact on the organization, according to Eliza G. C. Collins, senior editor of *The Harvard Business Review*. Speaking of liaisons between men and women of equal managerial status, she says, "This relatively new form of business affair is dangerous, because it challenges—and can break down—the organizational structure."[17] In a similar fashion, your relationship with your woman manager is also a sizzling time bomb, for co-workers can regard your romance as a danger to the social order. If they perceive themselves as her protégés, they may see the redirection of her affection as a true personal loss. If they feel distant from her and want a closer relationship, you're going to be viewed as a threat to their careers. As for the pillow talk between you, just imagine one of your peers fantasizing to another, "I wonder what he says about me when they're in bed together?"

When Your Boss Ends the Affair

Decision making for the complex issue of managers and lovers is difficult, because you seldom have a win/win situation, as Gail and Scott discovered. A top attorney with the Environmental Protection Agency in Washington, thirty-three-year-old Gail has been having an affair with Scott, a young lawyer on her staff.

Prematurely gray and quietly handsome, twenty-six-year-old Scott was hired by Gail soon after his graduation from Harvard Law School. The dynamics of their relationship affect her status in the office, and Gail decides to use her skills as a decision maker to end the affair:

Gail: I'm so sorry, Scott, but I can't join you on that trip to see the state's attorneys; the deputy administrator is showing a great deal of hostility toward me since he found out. In fact, he says he sees our relationship as a "major problem within the office."

Scott: But what about me, Gail? You can't just end it this way.

Gail: I'm afraid my job means too much to me, Scott, and as fond as I am of you, I feel that we're sitting on a time bomb, and it's going to explode under *me.*

Scott: What shall I do?

Gail: Probably it's best for both of us if I put in a transfer for you to the Missoula, Montana, office. I realize it's not the ideal place for your career to take off, but right now this is my decision. Please forgive me.

Choose Romance With Your Woman Boss or Another Job

Gail, in this brief conversation with Scott, shows you clearly why she has the position of senior counsel—she is a decision maker. In the resolution of a workplace problem that involved her professionally and emotionally, she weighed many factors before coming to a hard decision. These included her own career goals, her sense of corporate social responsibility, and the intangibles of Scott's future.

If you are ever in a position where you feel that your career is jeopardized because of a romantic workplace relationship with your woman manager, you might consider these suggestions for solving your dilemma:

1. At the risk of turning your beautiful love affair into a pragmatic business deal, suggest to your boss that you list the reasons—in writing—why your relationship should continue in its present state. Figure out what's in it for both of you, and write it out. Then make a decision.

2. Schedule an appointment to see a counselor who specializes in liaisons of this type. After he or she assesses the situation, write down the alternatives. What are they?

3. Try to view your relationship as a business issue rather than as a romantic problem. Take your mind off passion and focus on people—those who are most affected by your attachment. Is the company president or agency director embarrassed or hostile? Do your manager's other subordinates see you as a threat—someone who whispers the latest office gossip in the boss's ear? Is the workplace climate totally negative? If it is, start job hunting!

4. Could your woman boss receive a demotion or transfer because of your intimate relationship? When she suffers, will she blame you? If so, it's time for you to leave.

5. If you and your woman boss want to stay in the relationship, ask her to find you another job either with a different division or with a new company. This decision will save her career and start you in another—perhaps better—direction.

6. Make a valiant effort to distinguish between the decision you *have* to make in this situation and the decision you would *like* to make—given different conditions.

The Boss Who Mastered the Art of Decision Making

Ingrid is taking slow, deep breaths as she paces up and down in her colorful office. Surrounded by elaborate carved puppets from Indonesia, whirling dervish figures from Turkey, and ferocious wooden masks from Haiti, I feel as if I have just entered a gift shop of the United Nations. Instead, I'm in the offices of the Dance

Council of Denver, and Ingrid, their executive director, is about to explain how she became a decision maker.

"You're here at a perfect time—a crisis situation—the third one this year," she says with a rueful grin. "The Eastern European Folk Dance Company canceled their appearance ten minutes ago, and as usual, I have a real mess on my hands. Our concert hall is booked—a total sellout—2,800 tickets gone. Perhaps you would like to perform tomorrow night? . . . A Russian Cossack dance would be perfect!"

I'm aware that Ingrid is wound tight, but also that she is confident of her control of the situation. "What happened?" I ask.

Ingrid answers, "The troupe's artistic director had his visa revoked—something about his questionable activities during World War II. When the dancers learned of his plight, they refused to go on tour. So here we are, without a performance and a sold-out house; however, I have calls in all over the country, and in about two hours, we should have a substitute dance company."

"How can you appear so calm?"

Ingrid admits, "Two years ago, when I first took this management job, I became hysterical at each emergency. Then a very competent professor in the organizational behavior department of our local university taught me how to become a decision maker in a crisis. It was a 'continuing ed' series of classes, and it worked wonderfully."

I agreed with Ingrid that decision making is a skill that is vitally needed by subordinates as well as by managers in all occupations. She offered the following strategies that *she* finds useful for decision making during crises:

1. Before you make a move, take into account the way the problem looks from where you sit. This is managerial perceptiveness.
2. Decide on your approach to the crisis. Size up the dimensions of the situation, assess the risk involved, evaluate the degree of urgency, and determine who will be affected by the emergency.
3. Figure out the consequences if you can't decide on some

form of action. In Ingrid's case, she would have had 2,800 irate ticket holders storming the doors of the concert hall.

4. Judge your own persuasiveness in convincing others to approve your alternative solution to the crisis.

5. Psych yourself into a courageous mind-set or a self-assured attitude that convinces others that anything is possible! This means facing the issue squarely, bringing all of your past experience into play, ignoring your own frustration, and going about making your decision with confidence.

6. Make certain of your authority—whether it's clear, fuzzy, or marginal—before taking on the role of the consummate decision maker. If you have the authority, use it!

Boss Assessment Questionnaire: The Hesitant Decision Maker

Evaluate your woman manager for her decision-making skills using the following rating scale:

A—Always or yes	5 points for each A answer
S—Sometimes or occasionally	3 points for each S answer
R—Rarely or never	1 point for each R answer

1. Does your manager fail to convert her decisions into follow-through action by communication, committee meetings, interorganizational reports, or direct personal feedback to you? ______

2. Do you feel that your boss seems to pass up opportunities to take reasonable risks and thus fails to practice effective decision making? ______

3. After your manager makes a decision on some issue, does she always appear to waver, rethink her actions, and question whether she made the right move? ______

4. Have you noticed that your supervisor seems to operate almost totally autonomously—failing to consult with her peers or subordinates in gathering information about a problem in order to make a correct decision? ______

5. Is your boss inclined to keep all decision-making—both important and unimportant—under her control? ______

6. Does your boss appear to lack clear and direct authority from *her* manager, so that her role as a decision maker is never upheld by those in charge of the organization? ______

7. Have you found that your boss seems to "fold up" and become a nervous wreck when she has to make an early or urgent decision to solve a problem? ______

8. Does your manager ignore crises or emergencies in your department until the last possible moment and then proceed to make crash decisions that aren't always right? ______

9. Is your supervisor afraid to make the *best* decision to solve a problem if the decision is an unpopular one and doesn't have any general consensus? ______

10. Does your manager appear to actively dislike decision making instead of perceiving the need as an exciting challenge? ______

11. Does she sometimes permit personal friendship or political ties to influence her decision making? ______

12. Do you find that your boss neglects to give priority to what is most urgent among the problems facing her, so

that she ends up making a "federal case" out of even the most unimportant issue? ______

Total Score ______

60–45 Your manager epitomizes the stereotype of the woman who can't make up her mind!
44–29 With some assistance from you, your manager could become a decision maker. At present, her skills leave much to be desired.
28–12 Your woman boss will go far! She knows how to be a decision maker and risk taker.

Chapter 9

Breakthrough Women Managers

The Lure of All-Male Occupations

Breakthrough! The word itself resounds with excitement. Its definition—"a strikingly important advance"—reinforces our perception of an act of great magnitude. The unprecedented movement of women into the labor force in the last two decades has produced a new generation of managerial women—breakthrough women—whose progress in nontraditional occupations not only has changed the workplace but has altered forever our perceptions of women in business and the professions.

From politics to banking, from medicine to oil exploration, from publishing to law enforcement, women continue to enter formerly all-male occupations in record numbers. Each breakthrough woman represents a continuing struggle to move upward in a caste system where virtually all positions have been held by males. As more and more men find themselves competing with women, resentment smolders, for many men view these women as competitors with an inequitable advantage—persons awarded the job because of affirmative action.

"The resentment in the eighties is extremely subtle," says Beatrice Barnes Young, senior vice president of Harbridge House, a

Boston-based management consulting firm. "Years ago, it was okay to be openly racist and sexist. Now there is a collusion among both men and women to perpetuate the sexism quietly behind the scenes."

She explains that some white men are not able to accept the fact that a woman or minority person is "fast tracked" because of being better qualified. "When the man is passed over for promotion, he often will blame the affirmative action program for his lack of success," Ms. Young adds. "The only answer to this is for the business and corporate sector to implement management education programs to bring their biases out in the open."[1]

On the Street with Pimps and Muggers

In Los Angeles, policewomen are a common sight among the numerous patrols needed to keep order on the congested streets. But recently, about six weeks after thirty-year-old Gladys became a sergeant on the force, her all-male detail threatened a walkout. Pete, one of her subordinates, explains: "Most of us feel women should be home cleaning, cooking, taking care of the kids. They don't belong out here with the pimps and muggers. But, okay, they're now hired on the police force, so what d'ya do? For a while, we were willing to put up with this black broad, but finally enough is enough. If she wants the stripes that bad, then let her wear the pants right—with the fly in the front and quit bouncing people around like rubber balls. Sometimes she posts the schedule; sometimes not. Every once in a while she allows us a day off; other times she bitches when we request one. Occasionally, one guy gets a great assignment; other times, he gets the pits. What gives? Who needs a boss like this? She oughta go back to the kitchen where she belongs."

Juan, a curly-headed rookie with an infectious grin, struts up to us as Pete gripes about his woman supervisor. He puts in his two cents' worth: "I can imagine my girl bossing the other females in the beauty parlor where she works, but hell, Gladys is supposed to boss a bunch of guys twice her size. I think she's kinda scared of her new assignment and wants to show us she's nice by not yelling or shouting orders like my mom. But now and then, I wish she'd give all of us a pat on the back when we've scored. Like the other day, me and my partner brought in this two-bit crook. D'ya think she even said, 'Good job, guys'? Hell, no! She says, 'Bring in a couple more. What's one arrest. . . . You shoulda made three.' Then she walks out to get herself some donuts and coffee."

Coping with a Blue-Uniform Boss

Pete and Juan, our macho heros, are in a tough dilemma. They have a breakthrough woman boss who apparently lacks some basic human skills as well as management experience. Nowadays, few males will voice aloud their bitterness about working for a female manager, but for two blue-collar men who obviously prefer that women be kept barefoot and pregnant, the situation is demoralizing. Their boss needs coaching in supervisory skills, and unless their police chief is in favor of this type of active support for new women officers, the beat patrolmen will continue to be hostile and resentful. Says First Sergeant Malvain Perry, "Our big problem is we haven't too many role models. If you come from the Police Academy or the Air Force, as I did, and you're used to commanding, then you'll be okay with an all-male detail. But if you don't have this experience, you're in trouble. I personally believe that women in the police force need far more management training than they're getting."

Do you find yourself often upset and even seething inwardly because you report to a breakthrough blue-collar woman whom you feel has a negative leadership style? Are you boiling over because she lacks management skills and you suspect she's been promoted just because she's female? Then you might examine these tactics for coping with the aggravating situation:

1. Wait until your blood pressure is under control, then ask your vacillating woman boss to please post firm assignments on

a bulletin board or hand out a week's schedule ahead of time. Tell her you need it to keep your hours straight and your spouse happy. As you probably have surmised, inconsistent management sometimes is typical of an insecure woman manager. It's the one action that makes subordinates feel powerless, unable to control events by their behavior. Whether you're doing great or botching everything up, you never know what to expect next. For your own mental health, it's imperative that you speak up to help your female boss acquire a follow-through management style.

2. When your supervisor tells you that you didn't do well at your job, ask her what she expects from you. If you're in a blue-collar position—police, fire, maintenance, security—get down to specifics. What's wrong with your job performance? How can you improve it? What can your department do to help you improve? Show respect for your boss, but ask your questions seriously, and let her know that you expect an honest answer.

3. When you disagree with an assignment you've been given, bring it out into the open and discuss it with your manager. "A very capable woman boss is going to understand your position and try to handle your feelings intelligently and tactfully," says Commander Therese Rocco, the nationally known head of the Office of Community Affairs and Crime Prevention Programs of the Pittsburgh Police. "If I tried to overwhelm the men under me with orders, they would resent me. When I ask them to do something, I say, 'Would you mind . . . ?' or 'How about . . . ?' They might answer, 'That's a lot of bullshit, Therese.' Then I tell them, 'I agree. You're right—but the job still has to be done.' I don't believe that a woman in power ever should be like a colonel in the army."[2]

4. Try to be understanding and supportive of your boss. Remember, she's in a new and unfamiliar situation and is probably more uncomfortable than you. Bluster or defensiveness could be her reaction to an all-male environment.

5. When you succeed, call attention to it. Whether it's simply word of mouth or a few lines in your local paper, public recognition will add to your self-pride. Stroking is important for everyone, but if your boss tends to single out only certain individuals

in your department for special favors, this can destroy your faith in the reward system and play havoc with your ego.

6. If your boss or a woman in your group is pregnant and you feel antagonistic because one of you must "cover" for her, take a tip from Sergeant Perry. "I always tell the guys on my team, 'Think about her belly like it was a broken leg. Then you'd take over the extra duties without bitching. Right?' "

> "Wrong!" says Lieutenant Joe Olivera, a Miami law enforcement officer. "I had three pregnant police officers in my division last year and all they did was loll around the station with their legs up on the desk complaining about their varicose veins. Hell, they draw the same money as the men, and they aren't pulling their own weight. On the "narc" squad, it's dangerous for the guys, 'cause they don't have a real backup for a partner. There are great opportunities for women in law enforcement, but I personally don't believe females should walk a beat, be in a radio car, or be sent to the front line."

Anger, fear, hostility, and envy often surface when an all-male department reports to a breakthrough woman who, in their judgment, is not extraordinary. In some cases, particularly with blue-collar workers, anxiety and guilt are so strong that some men will hide the fact that they have a woman boss from their wives or girlfriends. Others will try "talking dirty" in front of their female manager, unconsciously hoping to intimidate or test her. A universal part of the male culture, such language is rarely used in front of a woman manager by educated, white-collar men who are subordinate to her. But locker-room jargon is still widely utilized as a way of expressing hostility toward a woman boss by blue-collar workers.[3]

Chivalry Is Outdated in The Workplace

Your ability to get along harmoniously with your breakthrough woman manager will in large part determine your own career progress. So obviously, it's time to abandon your knight's armor, stable your white charger, and adopt the proper—genderless—

business etiquette of the eighties. Miss Manners, known outside her nationally syndicated column as Judith Martin, warns, "Gender has no place in the workplace. The workplace is hierarchical and, there, rank is what matters."[4] So relax if you are a male subordinate, and quit trying to protect your manager. She's a breakthrough woman, not a damsel in distress, and this is what you should do:

1. Let her open the door and hold it for you if she reaches it first.
2. Shake hands with her just as you would with a male colleague.
3. Let her light her own cigarette, pour her own drink, and carry her own packages.
4. Allow her to put on her own coat, but help her if she's overburdened with papers and briefcase. In the reverse situation, expect her to assist you.
5. Leave the elevator immediately if you are at the front. It's absurd to plaster yourself against the side in order to allow your boss to exit first.
6. Let her hail her own cabs. Chances are good that she'll get one faster than you.
7. Step aside and let her choose how she wants to walk down the street with you. Protecting her curbside is no longer necessary now that she's off the endangered species list.
8. Compete with her for promotions just as you would with a male colleague. If an opening presents itself and you feel that your qualifications are superior to those of your woman supervisor, go for it!
9. Forget about standing when your woman boss enters the room. If you're in the midst of a conversation at the conference table—proceed. Your manager will find her way to the proper seat.
10. Tell your wife or special friend that you have a woman boss. Such a casual admission will deflect any raised eyebrows when you have to spend the evening at work.

11. Should she invite you to a business lunch and reach for the check, accept her gesture as natural. Put your credit card back in your wallet and offer your hand in thanks for a productive and pleasant hour.

12. If your ears are cold, keep your hat on when you come into the office. In fact, you needn't even tip it to your female supervisor unless you want to feel the wind through your hair.

Are Women Worthy to Boss Men?

Despite the influx of millions of women into the workplace in the last decade, the instinctive male response to the idea of a female superior is to doubt that she is worthy to boss him. These old attitudes die hard, according to Dr. Harry Levinson, management psychologist and president of The Levinson Institute in Cambridge, Massachusetts. "Men who want to identify with their more powerful male bosses often feel less a man for having to report to a woman. They're emasculated.

"In many cases," he adds, "the symbolic boss is a father or mother, and if the subordinate male is still dealing with conflict with his mother, it just complicates the relationship with his female boss—particularly if she isn't a superlative manager."[5]

From the more than two hundred interviews that I conducted around the nation for this book, I discovered that the men who appear to be suffering most from the flood of women into the workplace are those in what we call "masculine" jobs. Not only are they threatened by women who are their peers, but they are even more intimidated by females who are their bosses. Although only a mere 8 percent of all working men report directly to a woman manager,[6] there is still a great deal of apprehension if a man even suspects he's going to have a woman boss.

Prominent members of leading executive search firms corroborate this. Dr. Robert Jenkins, senior vice president and managing partner of Eastman and Beaudine, Inc., says, "Historically, the male has been considered dominant and superior in the workforce. It's a male environment, and men feel uneasy with a woman boss. She doesn't quite fit in with their style.

"Generally speaking, the skills of leadership are not the monopoly of the male sex but, on the other hand, men have a need for a comfort index in their work environment. They have to be at ease, do the things they want to . . . swear . . . make clumsy jokes . . . brag . . . let off steam. When their boss is a woman, they must stop and think, then change their behavior pattern. If they don't admire her competence, this compounds the problem."[7]

Breakthrough women claim they still feel the impact of male chauvinism, particularly from older males in senior management. A thirty-eight-year-old attorney who sees her chances of becoming a partner in her law firm diminishing each year says, "It's impossible to buck an invisible obstacle. The senior men in my firm and in others view women as lightweights—attractive ornaments to have around, but not as important contributors to what they call their 'frontline battles.' " Among 722 female executives polled by *The Wall Street Journal* and the Gallup Organization, close to half the women surveyed say that men at work treat them differently from male colleagues. Among these women, many more say this treatment is negative (71 percent) than positive (26 percent).[8]

Male executives unhappily corroborate these findings. "Chief executives who are my age or even a little younger still feel uneasiness in dealing with women," admits David Maxwell, fifty-seven-year-old chief executive officer of the Federal National Mortgage Association. He adds, "They're much more comfortable dealing with other men, for they're often quick to feel that the woman who is tough isn't being womanly, while the woman who isn't tough isn't worth having around."[9]

The Warden Is a Lady

Perhaps the most atypical workplace environment in which a breakthrough woman manager can be found is an all-male jail or penitentiary. Four years ago, thirty-six-year-old Anna Zaremba Thompson became the first female warden of an all-male correctional facility for the state of Connecticut. "I wasn't as concerned about being the first woman warden as I was about replacing a male warden who had been here at the Litchfield Community Correctional Center for over eighteen years," she says. "I had to win the loyalty of a staff that was used to his way of managing—throwing things when he was angry, challenging those who disagreed with him to a fistfight in the 'yard,' and keeping everyone in his place the way a typical old-fashioned warden is expected to."[10]

A striking blonde who modeled during her college days, Warden Thompson supervises a staff of thirty-five men and three women, plus a prison population of about one hundred inmates. She says she honed her present management skills working in a variety of subordinate positions—first as a guard in a women's prison, then as a counselor and assistant director of volunteer services in another facility, and finally as director of a criminal justice academy.

Coping Skills to Become a Breakthrough Boss

Adamant about the need for what she calls "in-depth" experience for both men and women who have focused career goals, Warden Thompson suggests you try these methods for developing your own managerial mentality—even if you are presently only in an entry-level job:

1. Be a risk taker, providing you feel that the personal and societal rewards are there for you.
2. Don't internalize mistakes that you make on the job. Correct them, if possible; apologize for them, if necessary; but don't carry them around with you as personalized baggage for the next year.
3. Keep your own personality! It's probably the best one for you, and if you attempt to mold yourself into the individual that

you believe the job demands, chances are good that you won't be successful.

4. When you finally have a staff—even if it's a staff of one—try to involve him or her in your decision making. An extra opinion always adds another dimension to your own thinking.

5. If you're a female subordinate, learn to make clear-cut decisions. "As women," says Warden Thompson, "we tend to see a lot more facts than males; we do more digging into a question, so we're often accused of 'waffling' on decisions." Start early in your career to become a confident decision maker.

Just how successful this breakthrough woman is in her "personalized" approach to management is attested to by one of her staff, Lieutenant Guy Oakes. "I don't even think of her as a male or female—she's just an extremely competent supervisor. The warden is tremendously organized, very self-confident, and totally fair. She never jumps to conclusions, but gives each one of her staff a chance to present his side and then weighs her decision carefully. The best thing is, she doesn't see the people under her as threats; she actually encourages us to take challenges and gives all of us opportunities to move ahead."[11]

Overcoming the Sex Bias in Medicine

They don't look like breakthrough dynamos. In fact, you might call them "grungy" in their rumpled, bloodstained green scrub outfits with the ever-present stethoscopes dangling from their necks. They're the nation's future women doctors—women who endure thirty-six-hour days, forty-eight-hour nights, thousands of cups of black coffee, endless trays of donuts, and in some cases more then a decade of special training to take their place in what was, until little more than a decade ago, male territory. In the brief span of fifteen years, their numbers have risen from 10.1 percent of the nation's 331,000 practicing physicians in 1972[12] to 17.2 percent of the country's 492,000 doctors in 1986.[13]

Until the midseventies, women physicians represented a barely visible minority in the workplace. Only a handful graduated each year from the nation's medical schools. The women's movement, promising emancipation from the feminine mystique, provided a unique opportunity for ambitious women to enter the profession in large numbers for the first time in history. Medicine suddenly became a coveted goal for bright, independent women who wanted a solid career, opportunities for personal growth, and assured financial security.

The phenomenon of women breaking through sex discrimination in the professions has had a momentous impact on society's perception of female work roles. Constantina Safilios-Rothschild, author and recognized authority on policies affecting women, says,

> One important attitudinal change that has already taken place is the increasing public confidence in women lawyers and doctors. These women have broken the sex bias in two masculine and high-prestige professions. The trust they now command has significant implications for women's further involvement and performance in these professions and other masculine occupations.[14]

Today, most major medical schools graduate classes of about one-third women, while the total number of women in residency training has more than tripled since 1970—a 335 percent increase nationwide![15]

Such a surge in numbers alone should mean that woman medical students and women residents are a welcome part of the scene in most hospitals. "Not so," says Dr. Nan Dunster of Sacramento. "Nurses in the intensive care units and in the operating rooms, in particular, tend to aim their volleys quite a bit harder at the women than at the men. I'm not sure just why, but I imagine it has something to do with the threat to their egos. In most cases, these specialized nurses are highly trained and more ambitious than their colleagues. They also have additional prestige, but every day, in every way, they are reminded that they are *not* doctors. And this is difficult for them to swallow, especially when they are teaching unskilled, inexperienced student physicians all that they know." By way of explanation, Dr. Dunster then told me of her experiences when she was first assigned to the operating room, or OR.

Unmask, Please

She says, "I was waiting my turn to be 'gowned' in the OR room during my fourth year at Stanford Medical School. I already had my mask in place and my hands—in their rubber gloves—folded at my chest. You see, in the medical hierarchy, the chief surgeon is gowned first and the med student last. Like the military—you always know where you stand! It's a courtesy code. Anyway, the circulating nurse comes up to me and I turn for her to tie my gown. Instead, she positions herself between me and the table where the already-sedated patient lay and says, 'Ms. Dunster, apparently you have forgotten the protocol of this operating room. You just touched your mask, so you've now contaminated our operating field. Kindly reglove and remask immediately.' "

Nan says she was bewildered. "I was absolutely certain that I had my hands crossed in front of my chest, the required sterile placement for the OR. I knew that I was nervous, but I felt very sure that I hadn't moved my arms. However, the circulating nurse is boss and you do what she tells you. So I tore off my gown and started all over. By the time I finished dressing, they were halfway through the operation and I got to see nothing."

Nan says at the time she wasn't sure why the incident occurred, but later, in relating the sequence of events to other medical students, she found that she was the latest pawn in the OR nurses' ongoing game against women medical students.

"All thirty-three women in our class had to regown any number of times when they were scheduled for OR. Yet none of the male students ever was accused of 'contaminating' the operating field. The worst part was that the men thought our unfair treatment by the nurses was one huge joke!"

As I listened to Nan's problems in the operating room, I wondered aloud whether sexual rivalry was a part of the picture. "Absolutely, it was everywhere," recalls Nan with a smile. "As interns, we were too doggone tired to do anything about it. But many of the nurses perceived us as threats to their relationship with certain doctors, so I'm certain that jealousy entered into their bullying tactics."

Jealous Women Bosses in Action

Dr. Carole Weaver, now a third-year resident in obstetrics and gynecology at a prestigious New Mexico hospital, recalls with a wry smile her first experience with this unforeseen harassment by a female boss in the hospital.

"I'm the daughter of a physician," she explains, "so I was well aware of the discrimination and sexism I would face when I was in a classroom with all males. Dad actually tried to discourage me from applying to med school. But I couldn't see any other profession. I had played with his stethoscope since I was five years old, always doctoring my dolls and any neighbor kid who happened to be around. I just anticipated two big hurdles—making it into medical school and then proving my ability to the guys in my class and the professors. But wow, was I wrong! Most career-oriented girls grow up with the sense of some prejudice toward women. You know, the the-men-get-it-all kind of mentality. But I never expected jealousy from women supervisors who were supposed to be helping me."

"How do the nurses show that they feel threatened?"

"In any number of ways," Carole says. "Generally, their actions are subtle, and often funny—unless you're at the receiving end. For instance, most women residents prefer to wear the surgical greens or scrubs that male medical students wear—that's the loose top and trousers—instead of the skirts assigned to us for the operating room. They're much more comfortable. But the only way we could get them was to ask the guys to filch a few extra for us before they went off duty. Then we would stuff them in our lockers so we would have them for the OR the following morning. Inevitably, when I came in at the ungodly hour of 5:30 A.M. to prepare for surgery, my scrub trousers would have disappeared—and a skirt would be there instead. After a few times like this, I finally asked the OR nurse if she had seen my trousers. She sniffed, tossed her head, and answered, 'Of course. I took them back where they belong—with the men. You're supposed to dress the same way as the nurses. After all, you aren't male doctors, so why try to imitate them?' "

Carole laughed heartily as she related the badgering that she experienced, then added, "The serious side to the problem is that it probably will continue until women comprise half of all medical school classes. Right now, the rivalry is intense and understandable. After all, the scrub nurse feels that women medical students should be scrub nurses. In her eyes, we are usurping her place. To make it even worse, we have to dress in the nurses' locker room. . . . Most hospitals in the nation still have only two locker rooms for the OR—the nurses' and the male surgeons'!"

The Psychological Cost of High Aspirations

Dr. Safilios-Rothschild sees this type of discrimination against breakthrough women as endemic in the workplace:

> Women who want and manage to achieve a high status, experience a "cold war" and must have the psychology of long-distance runners to endure the loneliness that comes from rejection by their colleagues. Many talented and hard working women have found the psychological cost of high occupational aspirations and achievements unbearable, and this has dampened their ambitions.[16]

According to Dr. John C. Myerson, chairman of the department of medicine at a Boston medical center, the rivalry between male medical students and highly trained nurses has been obvious for years. What is different, he says, is the unprecedented movement of women into medicine, which has given a new dimension to the traditional competition.

"Until recently," he says, "nurses enjoyed a special position as the only women in the medical hierarchy; moreover, they didn't resent being subordinate to the male doctor. After all, that was the cultural norm. Now, with so many women doctors, the highly skilled nurse in particular feels she has lost her stature to another female. Consequently, the only women who the nurses can lord it over—for a brief time—are the women medical students and the new residents. The bald truth is, both the nurse and the woman student are competing for the approval of the God-figure—the male surgeon. I see this every day, and I feel it's bad for both sides. Each needs the other for support in an environment that is still, overwhelmingly, a male-dominated enclave."

A Breakthrough Woman Manager

"The men I work with are the most chauvinistic, egotistical SOBs I've ever met in my life, and I would die for every one of them!" Special Agent Heather Campbell tells me this with the same gusto and passion that she brings to her job as a breakthrough woman manager—the first and only female group supervisor among the 2,500 agents in the nation's Drug Enforcement Administration (DEA).

Presently serving at Washington headquarters as chief of property management for the DEA, following twelve years as a street agent and two years as a group supervisor on the street, Campbell says, "It's not easy to be the first woman in an all-male profession. You have to love what you're doing and see it as a lifetime career, not a job."[17]

I ask the tall, slender woman what it's like to be in the vanguard of the 190 female agents who are now with the DEA, almost sixteen years since she made the unprecedented breakthrough.

Heather shakes her head in disbelief as she remembers. "At

the time I think the reaction of most of the men could be summed up by a comment I overheard just hours after I was commissioned. A tall, muscular agent was walking down the hall in front of me, and he turns to his friend and says, 'You know, I thought we already had enough agents on the force who didn't have any balls, but by God, now we have one we know for sure was born without them!' "

A Gun Is Better Than a Mother

Originally from Tulsa, Oklahoma, and the proud possessor of a master's degree in public administration, Heather says she always wanted to be a police officer. And that's the way she started—as the first woman criminal investigator ever hired by the federal government. She gently taps the gun at her side and explains, "In drug enforcement, your first line of defense is force, because the majority of the people we arrest are men—tough men. Generally, we sit around seedy bars drinking and talking. That's where a lot of drug transactions take place. I have to think like a man; my role models are men and, yes, I'm macho in my own way. Otherwise, I wouldn't still be around."

"How about your subordinates' reaction to their woman boss—do they find you maternal or nurturing?"

She responds to my question with an explosive, "No! I'm exactly like the men—I have to be to survive. You go to work one morning, and instead of being on duty nine to five, you're there for three days and nights. When you start negotiating with the dealers for drugs—it can take seventy-two hours until they finally deliver. It's hazardous work—you never know what's going to happen, especially when the dealers tell you they're going to check you out. The DEA focuses primarily on high-level drug traffickers. When we finally make a big bust, then everyone is relieved. We've all made it through another dangerous deal, and it's over, so the agents are hugging and touching each other—both men and women. Who needs a motherly boss?"

Sexual Liaisons Are Inevitable

I ask Heather whether she's aggressive. She fires back a firm yes, adding, "I might not sound aggressive, but I feel it inside and out. I have to make split-second decisions most of the time, so I'm decisive—a risk taker. Otherwise, how could I tell someone 'You're under arrest' and mean it? For that matter, how could I do all the things we have to do as special agents—surveillance, arrests, undercover work, testifying in court, negotiating for drugs with some of the most hardened criminals in the world—and not be aggressive? Yes, I'm aggressive, the way I want to be, and the way I have to be in my profession."

I can't omit a few more intriguing questions for this unusual woman supervisor. "What about your subordinates—any resentment from either the men or women? And where does sex enter into the picture? Surely, because male and female agents are together constantly, it seems inevitable that sexual liaisons would develop."

Special Agent Campbell says, "To answer the first part of your question, there is some tangible jealousy toward the agents from support staff. After all, we're the elite group. But women agents seem to receive a little more resentment from female staff members. As for the issue of sex—of course, you can't deny that it exists. The ever-present danger even adds a certain sexual excitement that might not be present in another profession. But it's a personal issue, and we trust in the emotional maturity of everyone in the organization."

Special Strategies for a Macho Profession

If the dangerous life appeals to you, and you harbor a secret yen to work in a macho, challenging profession like the Drug Enforcement Administration, you might want to look over this advice offered by Special Agent Heather Campbell:

1. If you have a woman boss, don't expect preferential treatment or a maternal attitude. Should you be a female yourself, your woman supervisor might be harsher on you than on your male peers.

2. Be realistic, and don't fantasize. A career in a profession similar to the DEA can be rewarding and challenging. But the job is also demanding, brutal at times, and physically rigorous.

3. Be prepared to approach your work as a lifetime career, not as just another job.

4. The DEA, or a similar organization, issues you a gun, a badge, and credentials. Special Agent Campbell says, "If they wanted you to have a husband or wife, they would have issued you one." A career of this sort is rough on marriage.

5. If you're a woman, don't forget, you're going to be treated as a highly trained professional, not as a female.

6. Make sure that you're secure in your personal relationships. The eccentric hours and excessive demands of this type of job mean that, at times, you're going to miss important celebrations like anniversaries, weddings, birthdays, or graduations—not the greatest way to keep special relationships intact.

7. Be prepared to be mobile. Special Agent Campbell says that in the DEA you can be moved eight or ten times in a dozen years.

8. Are you a woman? Assume that you're going to be watched a little more closely than your male colleagues, and you'll have to prove yourself over and over.

9. Although males might outnumber females by more than ten to one, don't expect this type of organization to be a happy hunting ground for husbands. When you're commissioned, there is an implicit guarantee that you'll be pursuing lawbreakers and drug pushers—but husbands, no!

10. Expect to like what you do or get out. Your life and that of your colleagues might depend on your commitment and dedication.

11. If you're attracted to a governmental entity like the DEA, be aware of the very exacting requirements. They include a college degree, vision correctable to 20/20, physical and mental fitness, and four to five months of intensive training.

Boss Assessment Questionnaire: To Become a Breakthrough Woman Manager

Test yourself to see if you have a serious desire to be a breakthrough woman manager. Use the following rating scale:

A—Always or yes	5 points for each A answer
S—Sometimes or occasionally	3 points for each S answer
R—Rarely or never	1 point for each R answer

1. Are you willing to be the first woman in a previously all-male occupation? ______
2. Can you take the heat if you're aware of resentment toward you by your male subordinates? ______
3. Are you able to forget your "delicate ears" and put up with locker-room language if the men in your workplace occasionally use it to express themselves? ______
4. Are you so focused on a career that your professional goals take precedence over your personal life? ______
5. Are you unashamedly aggressive in going after what you want in your career? ______
6. Are you assertive about your rights, and will you speak out if you feel you have been treated unfairly? ______
7. Are you willing to wield power in order to succeed in performing your job well? ______

8. Do you have a strong sense of self, so that you don't act defensive about being a breakthrough woman in a predominantly male profession? ______

9. Are you comfortable with the idea of bossing both men and women? ______

10. Are you exhilarated by the possibility of physical danger found in certain all-male occupations? ______

11. Do you revel in the public shock value of being the only female in a traditionally male field? ______

12. Are you always seeking new frontiers and looking for challenges that are not a part of an ordinary nine-to-five job? ______

Total Score ______

60–45 Your desire to be a breakthrough woman is overwhelming. Pull out all stops, and go for it!
44–29 You are venturesome, but apparently not 100 percent committed to pioneering.
28–12 Forget about trying to join this unique group of women bosses.

Chapter 10

You and Your Woman Boss—A Successful Partnership

During recent correspondence for this book, I asked Prime Minister Margaret Thatcher in what ways the fact that she is a woman affects how she sees her job. With incomparable British humor, she wrote back, "That's the question I always find very difficult to answer. I've never been a male Prime Minister, so I don't know what it would be like!"[1]

Mrs. Thatcher's wit notwithstanding, chances are good that if you asked your woman manager about the effects of her gender on her management style, she probably would reply in a similar fashion—but with a different twist. "That's a question I always find difficult to answer, after all, I've never been a boss before, let alone a male boss. So I have no comparison."

How true! Until the past decade, when American women moved into middle-management positions in sufficient numbers to become visible, the question of how to work for a woman was moot. Who had a female boss? If you were a member of the typists' pool and had one, she probably held the title "executive secretary." Traditionally, males have carried out the managerial functions in the workforce, while women have been relegated to "housekeeping" chores—keeping the office running smoothly, the coffee simmering, pencils sharpened, flowers watered, and the boss happy. For thousands of ambitious women, this now represents a bygone era.

The emergence of women into management has spelled the end of our stereotypical vision of feminine role fulfillment. With females currently filling over one-third of all management positions in the country, and with 71 percent of the labor force now comprised of women in their prime working years—from twenty-five to fifty-four years of age—there is, without a doubt, a major upheaval in the employment scene. If the trend continues, women could become a more dominant force than men in the management arena.

Dr. Janet L. Norwood, U.S. Commissioner of the Bureau of Labor Statistics, says, "What we have seen in the last two decades is a revolution! And we can never go back! In fact, not only will married women from a higher income plane continue to increase their labor force participation, but young couples who have gotten used to a certain family style of living will want to continue this standard—and that can only be met when both husband and wife are wage earners."[2] In other words, you had better not expect your woman boss to return to her former homemaker role.

Concurring with this view is Elizabeth Waldman, senior economist with the Bureau of Labor Statistics, who says that long-range projections indicate that by the year 1995 over 80 percent of all women aged twenty-five to forty-four will be in the labor force![3] What does this mean to you? Plenty! Based on the research compiled for this book, the phenomenon that Commissioner Norwood calls a "revolution" will have far-reaching impact for every one of you—male and female; entry-level subordinate to top rank management. There is no question about it—you *will* have a woman manager in your future. That is, if you don't already have one. If you have been reared in a traditional household, you will need to become accustomed to the idea of a woman supervising you on the job. For many men this is still difficult, for they must rely on role concepts provided by their mothers, wives, sisters, or lovers.

Young men in their twenties and thirties generally have far fewer problems than their older male colleagues in reporting to a woman boss. For some, it's a positive and enlightening experience. Howard Shapiro, senior vice president, law and administration, for Playboy Enterprises, Inc., says of his boss, Christie Hefner, "She's so bright and articulate—one could never find fault with her logic. She's also fair and consistent with all of her employees. Her method of managing is to hand you the ball and say, 'I hired you to do a job—do it.' The best part of working for her," he adds, "is that she's such a great role model for my children. My ten-year-old daughter, in particular, receives a positive message that a woman can be the chairman of the board. For her, it's a norm to see a woman in power, not an anomaly."[4]

However, older men from another generation are often blocked in their perceptions of the woman manager by innate masculine prejudice and corporate tradition. Says author Letitia Baldrige, "Men between the ages of fifty and seventy-five have to move out of the workplace in order for women to progress! They're still uncomfortable with women executives, and they can't see women making decisions in the boardroom."[5] Charles L. Brown, retired board chairman of A.T.&T., told me he would have no idea of how to work for a woman for "I never had a woman boss in my entire career."[6] In a similar vein, Milton Fine, chairman of the board of Interstate Hotels Corporation, explains, "The problem is that all of us are ill at ease in an unfamiliar situation. And, stated bluntly, we're just not familiar with women in the executive suite. We fumble, ask ourselves, 'Gee, what do I do now? How do I handle this situation?' And there isn't any easy answer, so we're all uncomfortable—both the men and the women—who must confront this new phenomenon in the business world."[7]

Not that being young, single, and male guarantees an egalitarian attitude toward women bosses. On the contrary, even though you may have an M.B.A., a female companion sharing your place, and a swinging lifestyle, your attitudes, like those of older men, are a product of rearing and life experience. One twenty-four-year-old called in on my radio talk show one afternoon and said that he had just quit his training course for flight attendants because "they are training too many women pilots"—adding that he felt unsafe because "women are too emotional to hack that kind of high-stress job."

As you have read in the previous chapters, stereotypes of women bosses still are prevalent in the business world, with widely held assumptions coloring our perceptions of female capabilities. A comprehensive body of research on biological and sociological factors of the female appears to demonstrate that most of the negative stereotypes stem from our upbringing as children. Yes, some women bosses *do* manage less effectively than men, listen in a different way from their male peers, fail to delegate, and sometimes have problems negotiating. But all of these perceived weaknesses are not a sign of inequality between the sexes, but rather an indication of a woman's cultural conditioning.

For instance, although accusations have been hurled at women for their lack of decision-making skills in the workplace, psychiatrist Theodore Isaac Rubin says, "Women traditionally have made decisions in families or in social relationships in one-tenth of the time that a male takes. Men ruminate and trust to a logical sequence of facts to lead them to a decision. Women bypass this type of thinking and trust their gut—the sum total of their experience."[8] The trouble is, now that women have moved into management levels in the workplace, they are fearful of using their so-called "feminine intuition" or emotional reaction to a problem, and so they procrastinate in order to postpone decision making. Hence, the negative stereotype.

In order for your woman manager to become a confident, effective boss, she needs massive support and understanding from you. This is not always forthcoming, as shown in a recent survey by *The Harvard Business Review*. Incredible resistance to female managers still exists, and women are aware of it. Almost half the women surveyed still believe that women will never be completely accepted by executives in corporate America. Four out of five executives still think that men would not feel comfortable working for a woman. And especially discouraging is the worsening perception of how women react to working for another woman—in many cases negatively.[9]

These attitudes bear out some of the comments made by men and women whom I interviewed. Says Dr. Robert Jenkins, "I think women don't like to work for other women any more than men do."[10] The crux of the matter is competition, claims Melena Barkman, assistant director of the Safety and Health Department of the United Steelworkers of America. The first woman in this position—a quintessential male enclave—Melena says, "People over you are threatened, no matter what sex you are, if they have the slightest doubt of their own competence. The men who are most uncomfortable with women managers are the dinosaurs—the older men who will never get over their male chauvinism. To put up with it, you have to stand back, not take it personally, and maintain your sense of humor."[11]

Lynn Williams, president of the United Steelworkers, and Melena's boss, is optimistic about the future role of women in organized labor despite their almost total absence in the management ranks. "One of the few things that is improving in our society is the role of women in the workplace—and that's wonderful. Remember, the principles and philosophy of the labor movement are that you're not supposed to have any prejudice of any kind. So with the powerful pressures from within, I believe that women will start to move up very quickly in the next decade. Life is timing—and the time is right for learning how to work for a woman boss."[12]

Edward Ritvo, group division manager for the American Management Association terms the movement of women into management an "evolution that is inevitable." He explains, "As men at a younger age become used to women in undergraduate and graduate programs leading to degrees in business, they will become accustomed to working *with and for* women. Thus, the resistance to this new phenomenon will dissipate. In addition, career-minded women will learn how to handle their subordinates successfully."[13]

In numbers, women have arrived. After all, you now have a woman manager! Equal opportunity programs and affirmative action have served their purpose. They spotlighted—at a necessary time—an issue that might not have been dealt with otherwise. But in the late nineteen-eighties, moving more women and minorities into the workforce is no longer our primary focus. Instead, your ability to work with your woman boss is the crucial issue. How do *you* resolve it?

From the start, you must be comfortable with the fact that you report to a woman. If you are a male, A. William Stockan, vice president for Playboy Products, Inc., says, it is up to you to learn how to act with your boss. "The responsibility to fit in this new situation lies with the men. We are the ones who created this system where men are in control of everything, and we shouldn't be all that proud of it. Now I feel we are obligated to help change come about. We can't wait for it to take place by osmosis or evolution."[14]

It is important that you are realistic in not expecting your female manager to be like the superwoman who led the way in the past decade. We have become so conditioned to expecting each woman who emerges on the national or international scene to be several cuts above the average mortal that we tend to be disillusioned upon discovering that our own woman boss is merely human. Edwin I. Colodny, chairman of the board and president of USAir, perhaps expresses it best when he says, "I don't think you can avoid the fact that the average male will have some feeling of awe toward a woman who's made it in the business world. We say to ourselves, 'God, she must be special to have gotten here,' and so we expect her to be a super performer. It may not be valid, but that's the way many of us perceive a successful woman today."[15]

Another point you must remember is that your woman manager is probably in a new situation. Because she has few role models to follow, she could be improvising new management methods along the way. If she was moved ahead faster than is customary in order to meet the affirmative action requirements of your company, then she is unsure of how to act and is possibly patterning her behavior after the men above her.

From the insight I have gained in writing this book, I believe that it is *necessary* for most women managers to adopt many of the characteristics of the successful male executive in order to succeed in today's workplace. This means that your boss probably has traits like aggressiveness, perseverance, competitiveness, and initiative. She undoubtedly is a risk taker and an effective negotiator. When she faced opportunities for advancement, chances are good that she took them, even if it meant transfer or relocation. To become an effective executive, a man or woman has to give work the highest priority—a difficult task for thousands of ambitious women who must fulfill several demanding roles. Of the top women executives, very, very few say that they have the time, energy, or the inclination to be nurturing, caring, or maternal. Virtually all of them maintain, as does The Honorable Barbara Hackman Franklin, that "leadership qualities are not a question of gender." The president of Franklin Associates and senior fellow and director of the Wharton Government and Business Program, she feels that women instinctively bring certain qualities to the executive position. "Women are often natural diplomats . . . helping everyone work well together."[16]

Echoing this perspective is Professor Janet Neipris, chairman of the dramatic writing program at Tisch School of the Arts of New York University. "Our greatest asset as women," she says, "is that we tend to administrate humanistically, working from both the head and the heart."[17]

Many of the executives whom I interviewed stressed the importance of support groups if you work for a woman manager. Outside of the office, it helps if you can share your experiences and confirm your emotions with those of other men and women who are reporting to a woman boss. The natural camaraderie and the advice you receive will be invaluable as an aid in sorting out your mixed emotions.

"Sometimes, it might be worthwhile to discuss your confused feelings with your woman manager," says Judith Wolk, director of marketing and development for Universal Trade Corporation. "I make a concerted effort to help any of my subordinates who experience problems in reporting to a woman. I'll assist them for a short period of time, then it's up to them to adapt and become comfortable with their new situation."[18]

Programs or seminars designed specifically to assist you in coping with a woman manager are nonexistent at this time. If you feel that it would be helpful, it might be advantageous to form a network among your peers who also report to a woman. The information and advice you receive may be beneficial in taking you through this period in your career.

Britain, in an effort to help subordinate women cope on the job, and to receive "a taste of a range of management skills," instituted several years ago an unprecedented program called The Pepperell Unit. Designed for both the employee and the organization, it is an effort to identify subordinate women with potential for management positions. It has been highly successful in bringing to the forefront some of the major problems that inhibit women's progress in the workplace. Included in the typical courses are a variety of training programs for women who must cope with problem bosses.

There is little doubt that you stand today on the threshold of a new era in the workplace. It is confusing, sometimes frustrating, but totally challenging. You are the pioneer learning how to work for the new woman executive. It is a novel experience for both of you. And it is vital—if you want to get ahead—that you recognize the growing need to be at ease with this new type of manager. As more women leaders become confident and sure of themselves, there will be less need to see them as "women managers." Instead, we will view them as "women managing."

Dr. S. Joseph Nassif, chairman of the department of theater, dance, and communications, and director of the Annie Russell Theater of Rollins College, says his years with a woman boss were among the most positive experiences of his life. "I once worked as producer to one of the most erudite, poised, gracious woman managers you will find anywhere—television personality Marie Torre. She was confident, self-sufficient, and motivated. When a woman manager has these qualities, you are indeed fortunate to be associated with her."[19]

Today, recognition of the impact of women bosses on the business world is slowly coming about. You can no longer ignore either their importance or their influence on your achievements and your life. The more we realize that we all must strive together for a compatible relationship, the more we can support each other in benefiting from this exciting revolution in the workplace.

As Prime Minister Margaret Thatcher wrote to me: "When you think of succeeding in the workplace, ask yourself—Why do people take the road uphill? Why do they climb Everest? Why do you climb philosophical hills? Because they are worth climbing and the effort is worth it. Because your feeling of achievement far exceeds the cost of the effort."[20]

Chapter Notes

Chapter 1 Women Managers Invade the Workplace

1. Patricia Clough, "From Boredom to Boardroom," *The London Times*, January 28, 1985, sec. 2.
2. Joanna Foster, telephone interview with author, April 22, 1986.
3. U.S. Department of Labor, Bureau of Labor Statistics, *Employment and Earnings*, January 1986, 155.
4. Federal Government of Japan, Ministry of Labor, *Annual White Paper on Female Labor*, 1985.
5. Yoko Koike, telephone interview with author, May 5, 1986.
6. Warren H. Schmidt and Barry Z. Pozner, *Male and Female Managers: Some Unexpected Differences*. An AMA Survey Report, AMACOM, 1983, 16–20.
7. Peter F. Drucker, telephone interview with author, April 10, 1986.
8. Anthony Astrachan, "Men On the Job," *Ms*, August 1984, 62.
9. Betty Friedan, *The Second Stage* (New York: Summit Books, 1981), 12.
10. Martha G. Burrow, *Developing Women Managers*, An AMA Survey Report, AMACOM, 1978, 8.
11. Ibid.
12. Bella Abzug, telephone interview with author, April 27, 1986.
13. Margaret Hennig and Anne Jardim, *The Managerial Woman* (Garden City, NY: Anchor Press/Doubleday, 1977).
14. Jeane J. Kirkpatrick, telephone interview with author, April 28, 1986.
15. Ibid.
16. Anthony J. A. Bryan, telephone interview with author, May 1, 1986.
17. Norma Pace, correspondence with author, April 30, 1986.
18. Jane Gross, "Against the Odds: A Woman's Ascent On Wall Street," *The New York Times Magazine*, January 6, 1985, 19.
19. Betty L. Harragan, telephone interview with author, April 3, 1986.
20. Wenke B. Thoman, telephone interview with author, January 17, 1986.

21. Jane Evans, telephone interview with author, February 11, 1986.
22. Bonnie Predd, telephone interview with author, February 6, 1986.
23. Susan Shank, telephone communication with author, May 6, 1986.
24. Roper Organization, 1985 Virginia Slims American Women's Poll. Results evaluated by the Roper Center for Public Opinion Research, 78.
25. Helen Rogan, "Women Executives Feel That Men Both Aid and Hinder Their Careers," *The Wall Street Journal*, October 29, 1984, 46.
26. Eloise Salholz, Mark D. Uehling, and George Raine, "The Book on Men's Studies," *Newsweek*, April 28, 1986, 79.
27. Bureau of Labor Statistics, "Employment Status of Non-Institutional Population 1952 To Date," *Employment and Earnings*, January 1986, 14.
28. Dee Davis Wells, telephone interview with author, February 5, 1986.
29. Wendy Crisp, telephone interview with author, December 11, 1985.
30. Felice N. Schwartz, telephone interview with author, February 20, 1986.
31. Charlotte Decker Sutton and Kris K. Moore, "Executive Women–20 Years Later," *The Harvard Business Review*, September–October 1985, 4.
32. Ibid.
33. Wendy Crisp, op. cit.
34. Jane Gross, op. cit., 68.

Chapter 2 The Manager Who Fails to Manage

1. Michael Korda, *Male Chauvinism! How it Works* (New York: Random House, 1973), 119–122.
2. John Naisbitt and Patricia Aburdene, *Re-Inventing the Corporation* (New York: Warner Books, 1985), 51–52.
3. Betty L. Harragan, *Games Mother Never Taught You* (New York: Lawson Associates Publishers, 1977), 35.
4. Sharie Crain with Phillip T. Drotning, *Taking Stock: A Woman's Guide to Corporate Success* (Chicago: Contemporary Books, 1977), 141.
5. Michael V. Fiore and Paul S. Strauss, *Promotable Now: A Guide to Achieving Personal and Corporate Success* (New York: John Wiley & Sons, 1972), 32.

6. D. C. McClelland and D. H. Burnham, "Good Guys Make Bum Bosses," *Psychology Today*, December 1975, 69–70.
7. Margaret Hennig and Anne Jardim, *The Managerial Woman* (Garden City, NY: Anchor Press/Doubleday, 1977).
8. Betty L. Harragan, "Advice: Ask Betty Harragan," *Working Woman*, July 1984, 26.
9. Rosabeth Moss Kanter, "How to Stop Being Stuck and Use Your Power," *Working Woman*, October 1980, 72–75.
10. Corrine C. Turner, telephone conversation with author, December 6, 1985.

Chapter 3 The Woman Power Broker

1. Katherine Graham, keynote speech at the 1984 Matrix Awards of Women in Communications, New York, April 16, 1984.
2. Ibid.
3. Eli Ginzberg, telephone interview with author, March 6, 1986.
4. Frederick Meinecke, quoted in *Machiavellianism, The Doctrine of Raison D' État and Its Place in Modern History* Translated from the German by Douglas Scot (London: Routledge and Kegan Paul, 1957), 405.
5. George L. Peabody, "Power and Organizations." Ph.D. dissertation, Union Graduate School, 1975.
6. Letitia Baldrige, telephone interview with author, February 17, 1986.
7. David Boddy, personal interview with author, March 9, 1986.
8. Ellen Gordon, telephone interview with author, March 10, 1986.
9. Michael Korda, *POWER! How to Get It, How to Use It* (New York: Random House, 1975), 42–43.
10. Rollo May, *Power and Innocence: A Search For the Sources of Violence.* (New York: W. W. Norton & Company, 1972), 109.
11. David W. McClelland, *Power: The Inner Experience* (New York: John Wiley & Sons, 1975), 93.
12. Rollo May, op. cit., 107.
13. Michael Korda, op. cit., 104.
14. Ibid, 105.
15. Aida K. Press, "Do Women Handle Power Differently From Men?: An Interview With David G. Winter," *Working Women*, April 1980, 44–46.

16. Edward de Bono, *Tactics: The Art and Science of Success* (Boston: Little, Brown and Company, 1984), 64.
17. Richard M. Ferry, telephone interview with author, March 5, 1986.
18. Heather Evans, "The Plight of the 'Corporate Nun,' " *Working Woman,* November 1984.
19. Rebecca Stafford, interview with author, December 17, 1986.
20. Dianne Feinstein, personal correspondence with author, May 3, 1986.
21. Diane Posnak, telephone interview with author, January 23, 1986.
22. Michael Korda, op. cit., 131.
23. Ibid, 151.

Chapter 4 When You Have an Intimidating Boss

1. Susan Easton et al., *Equal To the Task: How Working Women Are Managing in Corporate America* (New York: Seaview Books, 1982), 62.
2. Betty L. Harragan, *Games Mother Never Taught You: Corporate Gamesmanship for Women* (New York: Rawson Associates Publishers, 1977), 58.
3. George deMare and Joanne Summerfield, *101 Ways to Protect Your Job* (New York: McGraw-Hill Book Company, 1984), 81.
4. Jimmy Jones, telephone interview with author, March 7, 1986.
5. Madelyn Jennings, telephone interview with author, March 10, 1986.
6. Quoted in Joseph L. Massie and John Douglas, *M.A.N.A.G.I.N.G.: A Contemporary Introduction.* 3rd ed. (Englewood Cliffs, NJ: Prentice-Hall, 1981).
7. Rollo May, *Power and Innocence: A Search For the Sources of Violence* (New York: W. W. Norton & Company, 1972), 101.
8. Sey Chassler, "Executive Peter Pans and Wendys: Can They Succeed in Business?" *Working Woman,* September 1984, 168–69.
9. Peter F. Drucker, *The Effective Executive* (New York: Harper and Row, 1966), 168.
10. Nathaniel Stewart, *The Effective Woman Manager: Seven Vital Skills for Upward Mobility* (New York: John Wiley & Sons, 1978), 174.
11. Kay Cushing, telephone interview with author, December 3, 1985.

Chapter 5 Missing: The Ability to Negotiate

1. Margaret Neale, telephone interview with author, April 4, 1986.
2. Earl Brooks, telephone interview with author, April 5, 1986.
3. Gerard I. Nierenberg, *Fundamentals of Negotiating* (New York: Hawthorn Books, 1973), 12.
4. Blair Sheppard, telephone interview with author, April 2, 1986.
5. Earl Brooks, op. cit.
6. Mark H. McCormack, *What They Don't Teach You At Harvard Business School* (New York: Bantam Books, 1984), 149.
7. Gerard I. Nierenberg, op. cit., 4.
8. Edward de Bono, *Tactics: The Art and Science of Success* (Boston: Little Brown and Company, 1984), 180.
9. Jeffrey Z. Rubin and Bert R. Brown, *The Social Psychology of Bargaining and Negotiation* (New York: Academic Press, 1975), 172.
10. John Ilich and Barbara Schindler-Jones, *Successful Negotiation Skills for Women* (Reading, MA: Addison-Wesley Publishing Company, 1981), 16.
11. Elaina Zuker, *Mastering Assertiveness Skills: Power and Positive Influence At Work* (New York: AMACOM, 1983), 137.
12. Mark McCormack, op. cit., 3.
13. Gerard I. Nierenberg, op. cit., 3.
14. Margaret Neale, op. cit.
15. Roy Lewicki, telephone interview with author, April 8, 1986.
16. Roger Fisher and William Urey, *Getting to Yes: Negotiating Agreement Without Giving In* (Boston: Houghton Mifflin Company, 1981), 8.
17. Benjamin Fischer, telephone interview with author, April 9, 1986.
18. Herb Cohen, *You Can Negotiate Anything* (Secaucus, NJ: Lyle Stuart, 1980), 189.

Chapter 6 The Nondelegating Female Boss

1. Peter F. Drucker, telephone interview with author, April 10, 1986.
2. Katharine Graham, "Can We Have It All," speech delivered on April 19, 1983, Isaiah Thomas Award Day at Rochester Institute of Technology, Rochester, NY.
3. Nathaniel Stewart, *Help Your Boss and Help Yourself* (New York: AMACOM, 1974), 61.

4. Quoted in Don Caruth and Trezzie A. Pressley, "Key Factors in Positive Delegation," *Supervisory Management*, July 1984, 7.
5. Robert Maidment, "Ten Reasons Why Managers Need to Know More About Delegation," *Supervisory Management*, August 1984, 11.
6. Earl Brooks, *How Well Do You Delegate?* Technical Paper, Graduate School of Business and Public Administration, Cornell University, April 9, 1986.
7. Lawrence Steinmetz, *The Art and Skill of Delegation* (Reading, MA: Addison-Wesley Publishing Co., 1976), 16.
8. Earl Brooks, op. cit.
9. Small Business Monitoring & Research Company, "The Art of Delegation," *Small Business Report*, Part 1, November 1982, 23.
10. Small Business Monitoring & Research Company, "The Art of Delegation, *Small Business Report*, Part 2, December 1982, 5.
11. Peter F. Drucker, "Drucker on Delegation," *Management Review*, July 1984, 4.
12. Linda B. Downs, "Manager's Credo: Delegate, Delegate, Delegate," *Working Woman*, August 1980, 14.
13. James C. Harrison, Jr., "How to Stay On the Top," in *Executive Success: Making It In Management*, Eliza G. C. Collins, ed. (New York: John Wiley & Sons, 1983), 439.
14. Earl Brooks, op. cit.
15. Claire Gargalli, personal interview with author, December 19, 1985.
16. James C. Harrison, Jr., op. cit., 449.
17. Robert Maidment, op. cit., 9.
18. Eliza G. C. Collins, telephone interview with author, April 15, 1986.
19. Peter F. Drucker, telephone interview with author, April 10, 1986.
20. Ibid.
21. Lin Bothwell, *The Art of Leadership* (Englewood Cliffs, NJ: Prentice-Hall, 1983), 125.

Chapter 7 The Nonlistening Boss

1. William Ford Keefe, *Listen, Management* (New York: McGraw-Hill Book Company, 1971), 10.
2. Lyman K. Steil, Joanne Summerfield, and George deMare, *Listening: It Can Change Your Life* (New York: McGraw-Hill Book Company, 1983), 3.

3. Lyman K. Steil, telephone interview with author, April 16, 1986.
4. Lyman K. Steil, "Secrets of Being a Better Listener," *U.S. News & World Report*, May 26, 1986, 65–66.
5. Lyman K. Steil, "On Listening . . . and Not Listening," *Executive Health*, December 1981, 2.
6. Ibid, 2.
7. Joan Koob Cannie, *The Woman's Guide to Management Success* (Englewood Cliffs, NJ: Prentice-Hall, 1979), 109.
8. Lyman K. Steil, Larry L. Barker, and Kittie W. Watson, *Effective Listening* (Reading, MA: Addison-Wesley Publishing Company, 1983), 6.
9. William G. Callerman and William G. McCartney, "Identifying and Overcoming Listening Problems," *Supervisory Management*, March 1985, 39.
10. Carl H. Weaver, *Human Listening: Processes and Behavior* (New York: Bobbs-Merrill Co., 1972), 73.
11. Melanie Booth-Butterfield, "She Hears . . . He Hears: What They Hear and Why," *Personnel Journal*, May 1984, 37.
12. Ralph G. Nichols, *Are You Listening?* (New York: McGraw-Hill Book Company, 1957), 110.
13. Melanie Booth-Butterfield, op. cit., 40.
14. Ibid.
15. Lyman K. Steil, "Secrets," op. cit., 65.
16. Melanie Booth-Butterfield, op. cit., 41.
17. Lyman K. Steil, telephone interview with author, April 16, 1986.
18. John L. DiGaetani, "The Business of Listening," *Business Horizons*, October 1980, 40.
19. Linda Jane Colman and Susan Rawson Zacur, "Communication As a Business Skill," *Supervisory Management*, November 1984, 39.

Chapter 8 The Decision–Maker

1. Peter F. Drucker, *The Effective Executive* (New York: Harper and Row, 1967), 113.
2. Tressie W. Muldrow and James A. Bayton, "Men and Women Executives and Processes Related to Decision Accuracy," *Journal of Applied Psychology*, February 1979, 105.

3. Margaret Hennig and Anne Jardim, *The Managerial Woman* (Garden City, NY: Anchor Press/Doubleday, 1977), 27.
4. Luther Wade Humphreys and William A. Shrode, "Decision-Making Profiles of Female and Male Managers," *MSU Business Topics*, Autumn 1978, 45.
5. Theodore Isaac Rubin, *Overcoming Indecisiveness* (New York: Harper and Row, 1985), xiii.
6. Sylvia Senter, *Women at Work: A Psychologist's Secrets to Getting Ahead in Business* (New York: Coward, McCann & Geoghegan, 1982), 289.
7. Dale D. McConkey, *No Nonsense Delegation* (New York: AMACOM, 1974), 169.
8. Nathaniel Stewart, *The Effective Woman Manager* (New York: John Wiley & Sons, 1978), 122.
9. Eugene J. Benge, *Elements of Modern Management* (New York: AMACOM, 1976), 114.
10. Luther Wade Humphreys and William A. Shrode, op. cit., 51.
11. Robert M. Bramson, *Coping With Deficit People* (Garden City, NY: Anchor Press, 1981), 152.
12. James D. Johnson, telephone interview with author, April 19, 1986.
13. Marina vN. Whitman, telephone interview with author, April 18, 1986.
14. Jane Evans, telephone interview with author, March 12, 1986.
15. Christie Hefner, telephone interview with author, April 5, 1986.
16. Patrice and Jack Horn, *Sex In the Office: Power and Passion in the Workplace* (Reading, MA: Addison-Wesley Publishing Co., 1982).
17. Eliza G. C. Collins, "Managers & Lovers", *The Harvard Business Review*, September–October 1983, 145.

Chapter 9 Breakthrough Women Managers

1. Beatrice Barnes Young, telephone interview with author, April 22, 1986.
2. Therese Rocco, telephone interview with author, April 24, 1986.
3. Anthony Astrachan, "On the Job," *Ms*, August 1984, 62.
4. Joan Kron, "The New Double Standard," in A Special Report, "The Corporate Women," *The Wall Street Journal*, March 24, 1986, sec. 4.
5. Harry Levinson, telephone interview with author, February 4, 1986.

6. Roper Organization, 1985 Virginia Slims American Women's Poll, Roper Center for Public Opinion Research Report, 78.
7. Robert Jenkins, telephone interview with author, February 7, 1986.
8. Helen Rogan, "Women Executives Feel That Men Both Aid and Hinder Their Careers," *The Wall Street Journal*, October 29, 1984, 46.
9. Carol Hymovitz and Timothy Schellhardt, "The Glass Ceiling" in A Special Report, "The Corporate Women," *The Wall Street Journal*, March 24, 1986, sec. 4.
10. Anna Zaremba Thompson, telephone interview with author, April 18, 1986.
11. Guy Oakes, telephone interview with author, April 19, 1986.
12. American Medical Association, *Physician Characteristics and Distribution in the United States* (Chicago: American Medical Association, 1984), 12.
13. U.S. Department of Labor, Bureau of Labor Statistics, *Employment and Earnings*, January 1986, 175.
14. Constantina Safilios-Rothschild, "Women and Work: Policy Implications and Prospects for the Future," in *Women Working*, eds. Ann Stromberg and Shirley Harkess (Palo Alto, CA: Mayfield Publishing Co., 1978), 427.
15. American Medical Association, op. cit., 12.
16. Constantina Safilios-Rothschild, op. cit., 429.
17. Heather Campbell, telephone interview with author, April 23, 1986.

Chapter 10 You and Your Woman Boss—A Successful Partnership

1. Margaret Thatcher, personal correspondence with author, May 3, 1986.
2. Janet L. Norwood, telephone interview with author, May 5, 1986.
3. Elizabeth Waldman, telephone interview with author, May 5, 1986.
4. Howard Shapiro, telephone interview with author, March 26, 1986.
5. Letitia Baldridge, telephone interview with author, February 17, 1986.
6. Charles L. Brown, personal correspondence with author, February 12, 1986.
7. Milton Fine, interview with author, June 3, 1986.

8. Theodore Isaac Rubin, telephone interview with author, May 6, 1986.
9. Charlotte Decker Sutton and Kris K. Moore, "Executive Women—20 Years Later," *The Harvard Business Review*, September–October, 1985, 7.
10. Robert Jenkins, telephone interview with author, February 7, 1986.
11. Melena Barkman, telephone interview with author, March 22, 1986.
12. Lynn Williams, telephone interview with author, April 22, 1986.
13. Edward Ritvo, telephone interview with author, August 12, 1986.
14. A. William Stockan, telephone interview with author, March 26, 1986.
15. Edwin I. Colodny, telephone interview with author, May 1, 1986.
16. Barbara Hackman Franklin, correspondence with author, May 6, 1986.
17. Janet Neipris, telephone interview with author, April 27, 1986.
18. Judith Wolk, interview with author, April 15, 1986.
19. S. Joseph Nassif, telephone interview with author, April 22, 1986.
20. Margaret Thatcher, correspondence with author, May 3, 1986.

Index